The Stark Ranch of Cooke County, Texas: History that Spans the Red River

John D. Schmitz

Stark Ranch of Cooke County, Texas: History that spans the Red River

The Stark Ranch of Cooke County, Texas: History that Spans the Red River
Copyright © 2021 by John D. Schmitz
All rights reserved.

ISBN: 978-1-7367457-4-8

Library of Congress Control Number: 2021903641

Printed in the United States of America

Red River Historian Press
Lewisville, TX 75077

Visit Red River Historian Press at www.redriverhistorian.com

The information in this book is true and complete to the best of the capabilities of the author and publisher. The author and Red River Historian Press do not claim any liability or guarantee in connection with the use of this book.

Except as permitted under the United States Copyright Act of 1976, no part of this publication may be reproduced or distributed in any form or by any means, or stored in a data base or retrieval system, without the prior written permission of the publisher except in the case of brief quotations embodied in critical articles and reviews.

Publisher's Cataloging-in Publication

Schmitz, John D.
    The Stark Ranch of Cooke County, Texas: History that spans the Red River / by John B. Schmitz
        p. cm.
        Includes index.
        LCCN: 2021903641
        ISBN: 978-1-7367457-4-8

The Stark Ranch of Cooke County, Texas: History that Spans the Red River

Table of Contents

Table of Photographs	4
Map of Stark Ranch	7
Dedication	8
Introduction	9
Chapter 1 A River runs through It	13
Chapter 2 A Contentious River	28
Chapter 3 Over the River	37
Chapter 4 Connecting the River	57
Chapter 5 Starks at the River	72
Chapter 6 Roads to the River	82
Chapter 7 The River as a Resource	98
Chapter 8 Schmitzes at the River	108
Conclusion	114
Sources	119
Index	126

Stark Ranch of Cooke County, Texas: History that spans the Red River

Table of Photographs

1. Map of Stark Ranch. Red River Historian.
2. Colton, J. H., 1869. Texas with Cross Timbers. University of Texas at Arlington.
3. Brown's Spring, 2020, Red River Historian.
4. Marker at Brown's Spring, 2020, Red River Historian.
5. Mayo, George and Benjamin Harrison, 1887. Indian Territory. Library of Congress.
6. Delaware Bend Ferry, n.d. Tracks from the Past by the Gainesville Daily Register, Morton Museum.
7. Dallas Daily Herald, July 1858.
8. U.S. Army Corps of Topographical Engineers, 1866. Indian Territory. Library of Congress.
9. Dallas Daily Herald, December 1858.
10. New Orleans Daily Crescent, April 1859.
11. Cleveland Morning Leader (OH), November 1862.
12. U.S. Army Corps of Topographical Engineers, 1866. Indian Territory. Library of Congress.
13. Ranch in Cooke County, n.d. Morton Museum.
14. Ruffner, E.H., 1872. Map of the Chickasaw country. Library of Congress.
15. Texas General Land Office, 1868. Land grant map Cooke County.
16. Texas General Land Office, 1873. S. H. Brown preemption.
17. Warren's Bend ferry, n.d. Tracks from the Past by the Gainesville Daily Register, Morton Museum.
18. Ruffner, E. H., 1872. Map of the Chickasaw country. Library of Congress.
19. Permit Law of the Chickasaw Nation, 1876. Oklahoma State University.

20. Texas General Land Office, 1886. L. M. Ford preemption.
21. Indian rolls, Chickasaw, 1902. Mattie Overton and Edward Sacra. National Archives.
22. Texas General Land Office, 1899. Land grant map Cooke County.
23. United States Geological Survey, 1902. Indian Territory quadrant.
24. Scribner's Monthly, 1873. Bridge over Red River. Library of Congress.
25. The Marshall Messenger, November 1879.
26. The Marshall Messenger, January 1880.
27. G.W. & C.B. Colton & Co, 1888. Atchison, Topeka and Santa Fe Railroad Company map. University of Texas Arlington.
28. The Fort Worth Daily Gazette, November 1886.
29. 49th U.S. Congress Chapter 354, 1886. An act granting to the Gainesville and Chickasaw Bridge Company... Library of Congress.
30. 65th U.S. Congress Chapter 65, 1917. An act granting the consent of Congress to the Gainesville Red River Bridge Company... Library of Congress.
31. The Daily Ardmoreite, February 1919.
32. Sanborn Fire Company Fire Insurance Map, 1902. Gainesville. Perry Castaneda Library, University of Texas Austin.
33. City Directory, 1910. Gainesville, Cooke County Historical Society.
34. Census, 1880. Cooke County. National Archives.
35. City Directory, 1910. Gainesville, Cooke County Historical Society.
36. Cloud-Stark House, 1972. Texas Historical Commission.
37. Cooke County History Past and Present, 1997. Morton Museum.
38. Dallas Morning News, September 1978.
39. Toll bridge, 1919. Morton Museum.
40. Rand McNally Map, 1924. National Auto Trails Map. David Rumsey.
41. Harlow's Weekly, June 1929.
42. Unidentified ferry crossing, n.d., Stark Ranch Collection.

43. Toll bridge booth at Sacra's Ferry site, ca. 1931. Morton Museum.
44. Governor "Alfalfa" Bill Murray at Colbert toll bridge, 1931. Daily Oklahoman, Oklahoma Publishing Company, Oklahoma Historical Society.
45. Red River free bridge, 1942. Morton Museum.
46. Map of Love County, 1936. Oklahoma State University.
47. Red River free bridge, 1959. Stark Ranch Collection.
48. The Fort Worth Star Telegram, August 1938.
49. Pump station at Stark Ranch, 1954. Dallas Municipal Archives.
50. The Denton Record Chronicle, February 1954.
51. Gordon Street crossing, n.d. Dallas Municipal Archives.
52. Red River Authority brochure, 1960. Stark Ranch Collection.
53. "Participants in remarkable wedding and feast," 1919. Gainesville Register, Cooke County Library.
54. Gate to Stark Ranch, n.d. Stark Ranch Collection.
55. Gainesville Daily Register, July 1915.
56. Toll bridge, n.d. Morton Museum.
57. Gainesville Daily Hesperian, 1890.
58. Toll bridge ruins, n.d. Morton Museum.
59. Gate at Sacra's Ferry road, n.d. Stark Ranch Collection.

Stark Ranch and environs

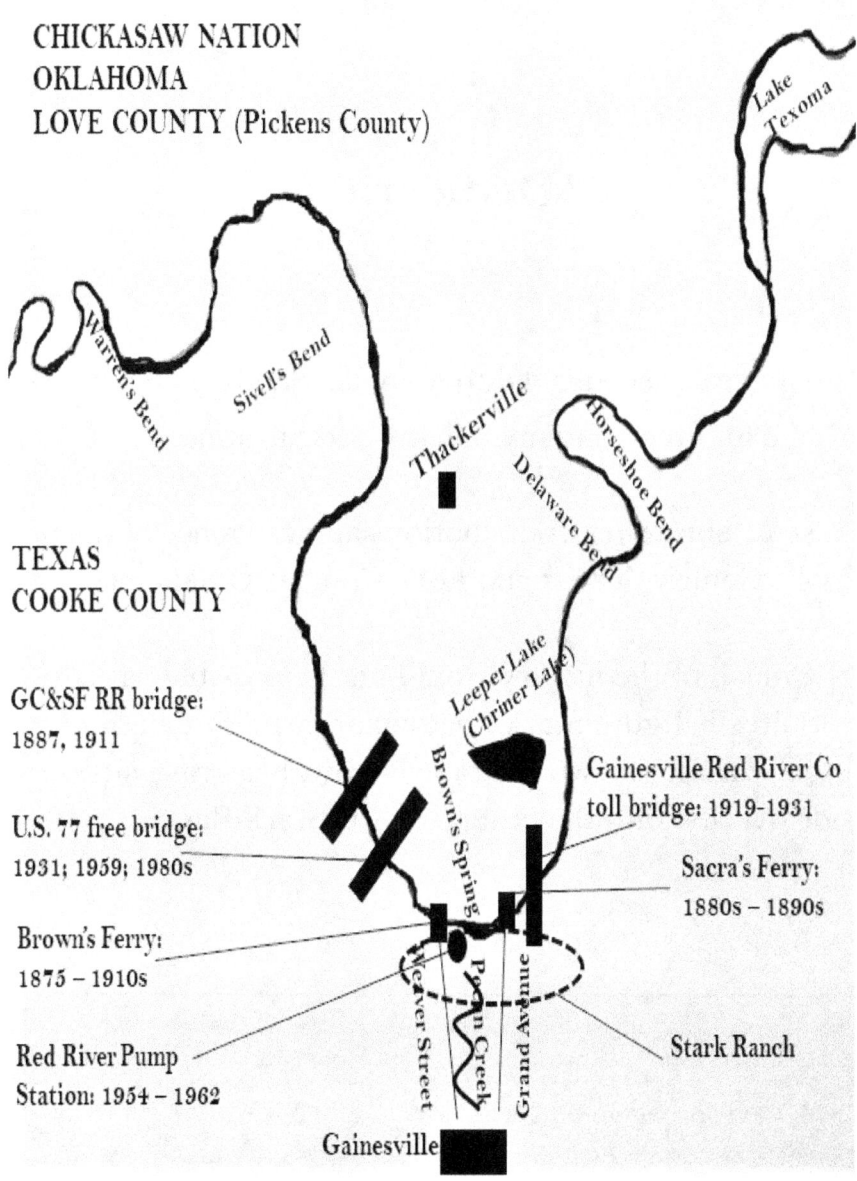

Dedication

These pages are dedicated to my wife, Sandy and our three beloved daughters, Tiffany, Shelby and Suzanne.

We also celebrate the contributions and diligence of the people in Cooke County, Texas and Love County, Oklahoma.

Lastly, much of the history would not be possible without Lucy Spires Killgore Stark, the tenant farmer's daughter who eventually came to own the ranch. Now, her grave sits on a hillside overlooking the beauty that is Stark Ranch.

Stark Ranch of Cooke County, Texas: History that spans the Red River

Introduction

Just off the eastern service road for the Texas portion of Interstate 35, a few minutes north of Gainesville and south of the Oklahoma border, sits a tangible slice of Red River history. On a dramatic hill rising high above the highway, the entrance to the Stark Ranch, a two-thousand acre estate, looks down upon the thousands of cars and trucks that daily drive along a road that connects Canada to Mexico and commands views of the Red River at its most scenic.

Once a historical conduit that linked New Spain to New Louisiana, and having served as an international border between Mexican Texas, the Republic of Texas, and the United States, the Red River slices through the southern bend of Oklahoma at the head of the ranch. Now owned by the Schmitz family, Stark Ranch is intricately linked to its historical geography; the very land itself reflects the people and events that bind the stories of the central Red River Valley.

The western Red River is an enigma in the American historical canon. It is the only major river in Texas that comprises part of the Mississippi River watershed.[1] But as the southern-most major river to connect to the mighty Mississippi, it proved to be the last documented. Until the 1850s, maps often referred to the Red River just west of Gainesville as "terra incognita." Early geographers vaguely described the area, and often did not bother to correct faulty information. Archaeologists have never found much interest in this section, and woefully few historians have devoted their research to the land and its people.

Stark Ranch's recorded history begins with land pre-empted and granted to S. H. Brown and L. M. Ford in the 1870s. Two ferry operations opened along the Bend; one was operated by Brown's family, and the other by Ed Sacra. Bridges eventually replaced both ferries. Both bridges extended from Texas into the Chickasaw Nation at Brown's Spring, a clean water source known by travelers for hundreds, if not thousands, of years. Comanches, Kiowas, and Wichitas camped here, and the springs became a known stopping place for Choctaws and Chickasaws who arrived in the area after the removals in the 1830s. The spring, sometimes called Refuge Spring, proved a magnet for outlaws, too. In fact, the whole bend area of what is now Love County, Oklahoma (formerly Pickens County, Indian Territory) witnessed violent crimes, many still

---

[1] The 1803 Louisiana Purchase included all rivers and streams that eventually emptied into the Mississippi River. The Red River is the southern-most major river that feeds the Mississippi. This means that the Red River was never part of Texas, which in 1803 was a Spanish territory and was not part of the Louisiana Purchase. However, the Sulphur River, which begins in northeastern Texas, empties into the Red River in Arkansas. Technically, this would mean that the land between the Red and Sulphur Rivers belonged to the U.S. after the 1803 purchase. New Spain did not agree to that. Instead, the U.S. and Spain negotiated the Adams-Onis Treaty in 1819 that set the Red River as the permanent boundary between the territories.

unsolved. Much of the crime derived from Texans who knew that going "to the Territory" aided them in escaping the law.

The Red River's history did not stop when the bridges for the Atchison, Topeka and Santa Fe Railway and the Hobby Highway spanned the waters in the early 20th century. In the 1950s, the City of Dallas built a pump station to send water from the Red River into the Trinity River and, eventually, to Lewisville Lake to counteract a severe drought. The scheme, which was ultimately unsuccessful, provides a glimpse in attempts at water and land management in Texas – and how nature can thwart even the smartest engineers.

The ranch draws its name not from the ferry crossings, the spring, or the bridges, but from a woman who made the land her own in the 20th century. Lucy Spires Killgore Stark, a daughter of sharecroppers from Arkansas, inherited the land from her first husband, William Killgore.[2] With her second husband Harlen Stark, their children, and the contributions of tenant farmers, the Stark Ranch became home to a handful of families. Lucy Stark was buried at the top of one of the ranch's hills, staking her claim to the land beyond the grave.

Within the pages of this book, the reader will uncover the broader history of the area as well as vignettes of life in unsettled and settled times. Stark Ranch, at the cusp of Cooke County in North Texas, encompasses almost two hundred years of Americana, from cattle drives to automobiles; from moonshining to casino gambling; from ferries to engineering

---

[2] William Killgore's last name is sometimes spelled Killgore, and sometimes spelled Kilgore, in newspapers and court documents. The authors of this book have decided to use the spelling that William Killgore used.

Stark Ranch of Cooke County, Texas: History that spans the Red River

marvels. The story proves once again how much history is hidden in places that Interstates race by.

Stark Ranch of Cooke County, Texas: History that spans the Red River

Chapter 1
A River runs through It

The history of Stark Ranch is intricately connected to the Red River and the primeval landscape surrounding it. Today, the river bottoms and the tops of the hills are capped by trees, some indigenous, most not. This is not how the area looked before European-inspired settlements arrived. North Central Texas and specifically, Cooke County, are historically framed by the Cross Timbers, a geographic phenomenon that writer Washington Irving once called "a cast-iron forest" during his travels in the 1840s.

Primeval Forest
The Cross Timbers are wooded areas, predominantly made up of "stunted" oak trees, that are not spread widely, but long and thin. The stands begin at the foot of the hill country in central Texas, wind their way through Oklahoma, and eventually reach into Kansas, occupying the space between the 97th and 98th meridians. Three long "fingers" of forest are divided into the Eastern Cross Timbers, which run east of Cooke County;

the lower Cross Timbers, which snake directly through the center of Cooke County and the Stark Ranch; and the Western Cross Timbers, which run through the western part of Cooke County. Interspersed between these post oak belts are prairies of tall Indian, bluestem, and switch grasses.[3] The roots of these grasses reach four times as deep as any tree roots, and they anchor the sandy and silty soils to the limestone beneath. The Cross Timbers are fed by narrow rivers and numerous creeks, with the Red, Canadian, and Arkansas rivers constituting their main barriers. These stands of trees act as the geographic transition zone between the fertile east and the arid west, and this role is reflected in the history of the region, too.[4]

Not much is known about the people who lived along the Red River in the Cross Timbers region prior to the 17th century. Migrations due to tribal wars, famines, and droughts occurred throughout the 13th and 16th centuries, when the large civilizations of North America, which built places like Spiro and Cahokia[5], decentralized and organized (reorganized?) into smaller family clans. Construction crews building U. S. 77 (now, Interstate 35) in 1940 found Native American burials;

---

[3] Texas Ecoregions. "Grand Prairie and Plains."
[4] Richard Francaviglia. *The Cast Iron Forest: A natural and cultural History of the North American Cross Timbers.* UT Press, 1998.
[5] Cahokia was the largest city in what became the United States in the pre-Columbian period (before 1492). Located on the eastern side of St. Louis, Cahokia constituted large pyramid mounds surrounded by thousands of timber homes in terraces that led to the Mississippi River. Further west, near Spiro (Oklahoma), was another major ceremonial complex. This city also had earthen pyramids, where the dead were prepared for the afterlife with elaborate tributes. The people who lived, reigned, and worshipped here were most likely the ancestors of the Chickasaws, Choctaws, Caddos and Wichitas. Both sites have been disturbed repeatedly by either grave robbers or by urban development. Spiro suffered a purposeful nitroglycerine explosion to steal artifacts. Interstate 70 now slices through Cahokia. Both sites are parks maintained by their respective states.

another Native American burial site was discovered at Delaware Bend through erosion, but a flash flood washed the remains away. While damming Fish Creek to create Moss Lake, burials uncovered in 1968 and 1988 were dated to around 1270 A.D. However, the tribal affiliation of the people found is unknown.[6]

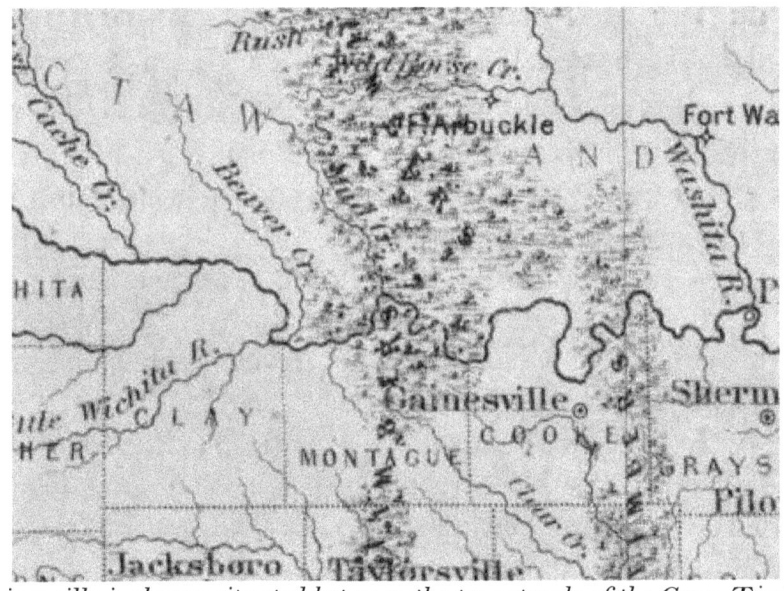

2. *Gainesville is shown situated between the two stands of the Cross Timbers in this 1869 map (UT Arlington).*

East of the Cross Timbers lived the sedentary and well-developed Caddoan civilization, descendants of Spiro, whose funerary mounds are still visible along the Red River's landscape. Nomadic hunter/gatherer tribes, like the Comanches and Kiowas, occupied the lands west of the belt. In between the Eastern and Western Cross Timbers, the Wichitas settled in villages and camps. The Wichitas comprised loose kinship groups who shared common ancestors

---

[6] John L. Robertson, *Cooke County History, Past and Present*, p. 2.

with the Caddos and forged hunting and trading alliances with the Comanches.

Just like the Cross Timbers marks a transitory landscape, the Wichitas who inhabited the space adopted their lives to this geographic transition zone. They lived in large villages around the rivers in the northern Cross Timbers and grew corn, beans, and squash. They also hunted bison and became semi-nomadic in the spring and summer months. In 1541, Coronado visited one of their major cities along the Arkansas River in today's Kansas. Coronado, a conquistador always is search for treasure, had hoped this village would be the mythical golden city of Cibola. Instead, he found a well-developed settlement of hundreds of grass homes named Quivira. In the ensuing years of their first contact with Europeans, however, the Wichitas began moving southward. This may have been because tribes like the Osages had moved into their territories and waged war against them, or because the Wichitas suffered decimation from Old World diseases.

The Wichitas
By the 17th century, Wichita-affiliated tribes had settled along the Cross Timbers region of the Red River. Since the populations of Native Americans had dwindled due to war and disease, the villages they founded in their southern territory included people from allied tribes, like the Caddos and Comanches. Through his second-in-command Rivage, Natchitoches-based envoy Bernard de la Harpe learned about these western villages in 1719. The Spanish visited one such village, Taoyava, in today's Montague County (Texas) and Jefferson County (Oklahoma) in 1758. The Taovayans had conducted a raid against the San Saba mission and presidio earlier that year. In retaliation, the Spanish sent over three

hundred troops comprised of Spanish and Tonkawa men, led by Diego Ortiz Parilla. The anticipated battle between the Spanish army and the Taovayan warriors was very short, as the fortified village, which spanned the Red River on both shores, easily repelled the attack. About a decade later, Athanase de Mézières, a Frenchman from Natchitoches who worked for the Spanish crown when Louisiana came under Spanish jurisdiction after 1763, visited the villages. He established friendship with the Taovayans while at the same time claiming them for Spain; he named the western (Texas) village San Bernardo, and the eastern (Oklahoma) village San Teodoro.[7] By the 1830s, the Taovayan villagers had resettled further upstream at the base of the Wichita Mountains after a devastating smallpox outbreak.[8]

The original Taovayan village, less than one hundred miles from the deep, southward bend of the river which Stark Ranch now occupies, appears to have been the only Native American settlement situated directly on the river in the western Red River valley. Subsequent Anglo explorers who came to the western Red River Valley after the Louisiana Purchase of 1803 reference another settlement at the river's edges, but its location is yet unrevealed.[9]

---

[7] According to Spanish accounts, a French flag flew above the village, which was surrounded by a wooden fort and fields of squash, melons, and pumpkins. Over two thousand people lived here in tents and grass houses.

[8] In 1834, the famous artist George Catlin visited the relocated Wichita village at the base of the Wichita mountains with the Dodge-Leavenworth expedition and produced a pencil sketch of it.

[9] In 1816, Englishman Henry Ker self-published a travelogue of his journey up the Red Rive after he explored the river in search of treasure. For some reason, his accounts have been dismissed by a 19th century scholar as "fanciful" and "most likely untrue" although he does not explain why. Subsequent historians have thus summarily dismissed his writings. Therefore, his claim of a large settlement near the Red River on the right side (Oklahoma) has not been researched at all.

The history of the western Red River and of Stark Ranch in particular, then, begins with American settlement.

3. Brown's Spring, named for Texas land grantee S.H. Brown and his family, sits across from Stark Ranch (Red River Historian).

The Spring

The Red River originates in the Texas panhandle, an arid semi-desert region. It starts as a large spring that cuts through gypsum cliffs and sandstone, making its waters undrinkable. But in Love County at the base of the dramatic southward drop and the near vertical northward flow of the Red River at the head of Stark Ranch, is a clean water spring that has served travelers for centuries. This place has been named Brown's Spring for its ties to A.W. Brown, the ferry operator on the Texas side of the spring and a brother to land grantee S.H. Brown. Early settlers called it Refuge Springs.

Recorded accounts of the spring do not appear until the 1930s, when passing references are made in oral histories of early settlers in Indian Territory. Their descriptions of the spring illuminate that it may have served as a way marker for

4. *Marker at Brown's Spring Cemetery (Red River Historian).*

travelers. In her oral history interview, Lillie Sprowls remembers that when living at Brown's Spring as a child, she had "dug up all kinds of dishes and some human bones."[10] By the 1860s, the Criners, a Chickasaw family who had lived down river at Colbert, settled the land at Brown's Spring. There, they established a small store and a cemetery where the first grave was dug in 1867. A town called Texanna appeared just north of the spring in the 1870s, but inhabitants moved to Thackerville (which itself had moved) to be closer to the railroad.[11]

---

[10] Indian Pioneer Papers, "Lillie Sprowls," 1937.
[11] ibid

Stark Ranch of Cooke County, Texas: History that spans the Red River

In the two decades prior to the Civil War, Chickasaws, Choctaws, Anglo-American and European emigrants to Texas, soldiers, and traders slowly began to populate the central portion of the Red River Valley. Though not yet an incorporated city, Gainesville beckoned as a potential economic hub at the far reaches of the Texas frontier. These varied people did not cross the Red River at Brown's Spring, however, as the hills that hugged both sides of the river proved too steep. They either crossed near Abel Warren's trading post west of Brown's Spring; forded the river west of the deep bend at Stark Ranch or east at Addington Bend; or took Colbert's Ferry several miles east, the safest route.[12] Due to the lack of a north/south thoroughfare between Gainesville and Indian Territory, this area remained fairly isolated until the Brown and Sacra ferries began operating in the 1870s and 1880s. The isolation offered an opportunity for outlaws to hide in the thickets of today's Love County, including moonshiners, who by law were forbidden to operate or sell whiskey in any part of the Chickasaw Nation. To enforce the laws and provide protection from seedier elements, the U.S. Army founded Fort Washita in today's Bryan County, Oklahoma in 1847 and Fort Arbuckle in today's Johnson County, Oklahoma in 1854. Fort Fitzhugh, built by Texas Rangers southeast of Gainesville in

---

[12] A Chickasaw citizen, Benjamin Colbert opened a ferry station along the Red River between today's Bryan County, Oklahoma and Grayson County, Texas to replicate the operation he had founded in Mississippi before he and his family removed to Indian Territory in the 1830s. Colbert quickly regained his prosperity in the Indian Territory as he located his ferry, farm, ranch, and hotel along the Texas Road, an emigrant trail that connected Fort Scott (AR) to southern Indian Territory, witnessed the cattle drives to Sedalia, and served as a route on the Butterfield Overland Stagecoach. The site of his ferry operation would become a toll bridge, financed by the Red River Bridge Company in the early 20th century, and by the 1930s, it centered the free/toll bridge controversy between Texas and Oklahoma, which will be explored later in the book.

1847 to protect white settlers from raids, closed in the 1850s when its location proved irrelevant.

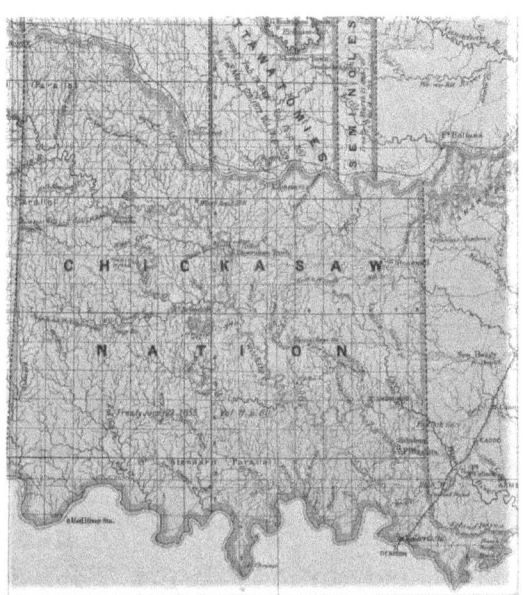

5. *The Chickasaw Nation was established in the 1850s and carved from the Choctaw Nation (1887, Library of Congress).*

The Chickasaws

The Chickasaws arrived in the Red River area at Brown's Spring in the 1840s and 1850s. The tribe, originally from Kentucky and Tennessee, constituted one of the "Five Civilized Tribes" whom the Indian Removal Act of 1830 affected. Like the Choctaws, Cherokees, Seminoles, and Creeks, the Chickasaws endured a trail of tears to reach Indian Territory. Unlike the other tribes, though, their journeys varied greatly. In 1818, the Chickasaws signed the Treaty of Old Town, the first removal treaty that resettled them in Alabama and Mississippi. In the ensuing years, some Chickasaws married white people and adopted southern habits, including chattel slavery and cash crop agriculture. When subsequent treaties sought to move them into Indian Territory but without equitable land exchanges, the half-white Chickasaw families who owned land individually sold their lands privately instead. Consequently, "full blood" Chickasaws who held their land communally suffered greater privation than the private holders, and this wealth disparity replicated itself in Indian Territory.

The Chickasaws settled in the western half of the Choctaw Nation. In 1855, the Chickasaws signed a treaty which created their own government separate from the Choctaws. After paying the Choctaws for the western half of the lands which was known as the Chickasaw District, the tribe founded their new government at Tishomingo. The district had been subdivided into counties by the Choctaws. When the Chickasaws moved into the district in large numbers, the Choctaws renamed the counties to reflect Chickasaw heritage. In 1854, Brown's Spring and Love Valley became part of Pickens County of the Chickasaw Nation, which replaced Wichita County of the Choctaw Nation. The county was named in honor of Edmund Pickens, the first elected chief of the Chickasaw Nation in Indian Territory. His Chickasaw name was Okchantubby.[13]

Wealthier citizens had the money and resources to claim vast tracts of lands that the tribe had leased from the Choctaws in anticipation of founding their own nation upon the completed compensation of all their eastern lands. Some of the land was sold or pre-empted by non-Chickasaw men. Gradually, the Chickasaw nation became known for large ranching operations; by 1866, the Addington, Cloud, McLish,

---

[13] Juanita J. Keel Tate. *Edmund Pickens (Okchantubby): First elected Chickasaw Chief, his life and times.* Chickasaw Press, 2009.

Fleetwood, Love, and Sugg ranches occupied huge swaths of lands in the Red River Valley.

The Delawares and the Shawnees

Other Native American tribes moved into the Red River Valley between 1815 and 1865; unlike the Chickasaws who signed removal treaties in exchange for land, the Shawnees and Delawares who came to the Red River Valley were essentially refugees.

The Shawnees had been forced from their homelands in the Ohio River Valley after the Shawnee War of 1811. The tribe dispersed west of the Mississippi, and about a hundred Shawnees sought land claims in Mexican Texas along the Red River. Once there, they built several small villages which were labeled generically as "Shawnee Towns" on maps. One of the Shawnee Towns sat opposite Colbert's Ferry on the Red River (between Denison, Texas and Durant, Oklahoma).

The same fate of the Shawnees befell some of the Delawares. Originally from the Delaware River area on the eastern U.S. seaboard, the tribe signed removal treaties that led them to the Ohio River Valley. They lost their new homelands after 1811 and subsequently applied for land grants in Mexican Texas. Like the Shawnees, the Delawares established small settlements which contemporary maps simply marked as "Delaware." One of their settlements became known as Delaware Bend, which juts along the Red River in Cooke County northeast of Stark Ranch.[14]

---

[14] The land grants made to the Shawnees and Delawares by the Spanish and Mexican governments were never completed. Subsequently, the Republic of Texas did not honor the grants (the U.S. government did not recognize land grants to Native Americans at all). Shawnee Town at Colbert's Ferry was an exception; Anglo settlers paid the

Cooke County

Ranching and farming operations emerged on the southern banks of the Red River, too. The Texas legislature cleaved Cooke County from Grayson County in 1848, and Gainesville became its county seat. The early town site hugged the banks of Pecan Creek, a stream that originates inside the

6. *Gainesville residents at the Delaware Bend Ferry crossing in the early 20th century (Morton Museum).*

Stark Ranch holdings. The state gave the Peter's Colony Land Grant Company a charter to sell whatever titles they could in northeastern Texas, which included Cooke County. Not many of the Anglo settlers in Cooke County took advantage of the Peter's Colony land grants. Instead, they simply settled the land and began improving it without acquiring title. Emigrants came from Arkansas, Tennessee, New York, Indiana, Kentucky, Missouri, and Texas. A few of the settlers replicated the southern slave-holding system in the plantations and ranches they founded; however, settlers tended to be

---

Shawnees to leave their settlement, which became Red River City, founded by the Houston and Texas Central Railway in 1872. Subsequently, the dispossessed Shawnees and Delawares found homes in Indian Territory and are now federally recognized tribes.

small-time farmers and tradesmen who did not own other people. They set their homesteads on Comanche territorial claims, and raids against their settlements often proved deadly for both sides.

Texas, of course, ignored the Comanche territorial claims and Anglo Texans actively sought tribal destruction. Cooke County residents William C. Young commandeered the Third Texas Mounted Volunteers during the Mexican-American War (1846-1848), and James Bourland served as his second-in-command. Both men had become substantial landowners

> The Peters' Colony Commissioners met on Monday the 28th ult. at Fort Worth, Tarrant county. They found that 26 certificates had been issued since Feb. 1855, of which 14 were approved. The Board met at Gainesville, Cooke county, on Monday the 5th inst. Seventy-five certificates had been issued by the County court since August 1855, of which nine only were approved. There was a full Board at both places. The Board will meet at McKinney, Collin county on the 26th inst.

7. Peter's Colony in Cooke County was not very successful
(Dallas Daily Herald, July 1858, Newspapers.com)

along the Red River east of the Stark Ranch in Cooke County on the eve of the Civil War, and both men conducted war against Comanches, Caddos, and Wichitas. In 1858, Bourland organized a Ranger force at Gainesville "for the protection of the Northern frontier against the depredations of hostile bands of Indians that have recently come across the Red River and committed murder and thefts."[15] These Ranger outfits seemed to do more harm than good; residents in Young County, west

---

[15] Dallas Daily Herald, October 27 1858.

of Cooke County, reported that the "rangers were as bad as the Indians are said to be."[16]

Despite frontier troubles, whether real or imagined, Cooke County grew exponentially in the 1850s. By 1858, Gainesville received mail three times weekly and was also on the route on the route of the Butterfield Overland Stagecoach and Mail Company, the first transcontinental stagecoach that linked St. Louis to San Diego. Gainesville became a trading center for bison, deer, and cow hides coming down from the "Whiskey Trail," a moon-shiner's path that linked the Arbuckle mountains to Cooke County.[17] This trail was considered quite

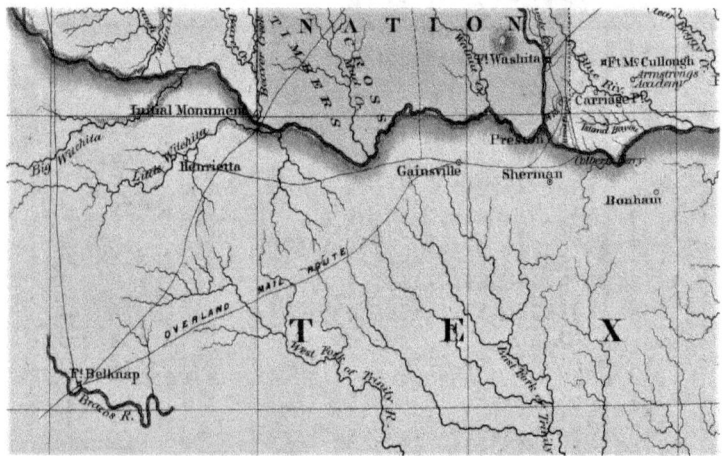

8. Gainesville served as a stop between Sherman and Fort Belknap for the Butterfield Overland Stagecoach and Mail Route Company (1866, Library of Congress).

---

[16] Dallas Daily Herald, July 13 1859.

[17] Indian Pioneer Papers. "R. L. Nichols" and "Dixie Colbert." (1937). According to Henry M. Brown's interview for the WPA, the trail was blazed by Colonel Bourland. The "Whiskey Trail" was labeled as the "Indian Trail" by the U.S. military in a map dated 1866 and became known as the Gainesville Road in a map from 1872. The whiskey flowed northward; Texas moonshiners sold it to people in Indian Territory, as the liquor trade was forbidden by the Chickasaw Nation.

dangerous to travel by night due to the bootleggers. Almost four thousand people called Cooke County home in 1860.

On the eve of the Civil War, the Red River Valley along the Love Valley bend grew into a busy, prosperous, and often, a lawless place.

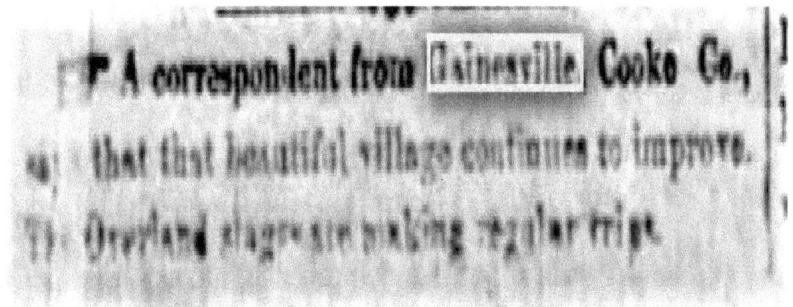
9. *Butterfield Stagecoach notice at Gainesville in the Dallas Daily Herald, December 1858 (Newspapers.com).*

Chapter 2
A Contentious River

The Civil War did not come to Cooke County easily. Sixty-one percent of Cooke County white men voted against secession in 1861 but slavery was far from frowned upon. The county, which in 1860 numbered three thousand three hundred and ninety one people, had an enslaved population of eleven percent.[18] Comparative numbers between the 1850 and 1860 censuses indicate that slave-owning was a lucrative business for a select group of people. In the 1850 census for Cooke County, one white man owned one black man. Within ten years, the percentage went to twenty-three white people owning three-hundred and eighty-nine black people — less than one percent of the entire white population owned people, but they held extraordinary power.[19]

---

[18] 1860 Census, tabulated.
[19] ibid

> These preachers have been notified to leave, and from the character of the demonstration at Bonham, they will be likely to conclude that the people are fully aroused against them. The Independent states that nearly every county in the State has one or more of these abolition emissaries of the Northern Methodist church. We are inclined to believe this statement true. These men should not be tolerated in slaveholding communities, and we trust they will be ferreted out, and dealt with as they justly deserve.

10. An editorial in the New Orleans Daily Crescent from April 1859 warns against abolitionists (Newspapers.com).

"Texas Troubles" in Cooke County

When people traffic in other humans, there is inevitably a moral quandary, and this spilled over into defensive rumor-mongering. Historians call this the "Texas Troubles," a period of time during the conflict in Kansas when Texans believed abolitionists and slaves were conspiring to murder white slave owners. In North Texas, the accusations of "outside agitators" instigating violence and murder plots came to a fever pitch in 1859. The New Orleans Crescent reported that "abolitionists have insinuated themselves" in the Northern Methodist congregation in Fannin County. "Every county in the state," the article stated, "has one of more of these abolition emissaries… these men should not be tolerated in slaveholding communities."[20] A newspaper article from the *Dallas Daily Herald* related that a man named George Humphries, who lived in Gainesville and worked for the Butterfield Overland Stagecoach Company, removed from Cooke County in 1859 and left a stash of letters behind. One of Humphries' correspondents was E. C. Palmer, a fellow New Yorker who lived near Marshall, Texas. His letter, published by the Herald, hoped that "we will have a general war soon between

---

[20] New Orleans Daily Crescent, April 13 1859.

the North and South" and that "we will have to kill them off before we can have a peaceful government." A Henderson County court believed that Palmer and Humphries were trying to bring the Kansas conflict to North Texas.[21] Both Henderson and Cooke Counties "solemnly pledge(d) ourselves to use every means in our reach to remove such person from among us."[22] S.M. Doss, one of the county's largest slave-owners, chaired the committee that resolved to "request [Palmer] to depart from our midst within six hours… in the event of his failure to do so, he will be rode upon a rail."[23]

In the 1850s and 1860s, Anglo settlement concentrated in the eastern portions of the county; just west of Gainesville stood

---

[21] In 1858, the territories of Kansas and Nebraska were becoming populated by enough U.S. citizens that they verged on forming states. Since they originated from the Louisiana Territory, the Missouri Compromise of 1820 applied to their state creation. This meant that, since both Kansas and Nebraska were situated above the 36th parallel, they must enter the United States as free (non-slave) states. However, in 1848, the United States had acquired the Mexican Cession, which included California. California had enough people already to form a state in 1850. If the Missouri Compromise had been extended to the former Mexican lands, then the southern half of California could have technically become a slave state; however, the Treaty of Hidalgo between the United States and Mexico prohibited the enslavement of former Mexican nationals, and California was in no way interested in becoming a slave state. Basically, this meant that no territory west of Texas or north of Indian Territory could become slave states, thus prohibiting the spread and influence of the slave-system. Southern states were in an uproar. In 1854, Congress passed the Kansas-Nebraska Act, which stipulated that Kansas and Nebraska territories could decide for themselves if they wanted to enter as free or slave states, thus nullifying the Missouri Compromise. Abolitionists, like John Brown, from all over the United States moved into Kansas to vote in its constitutional convention; slavers from Missouri, like Jesse James, led raids into the Kansas Territory to terrorize the abolitionists. Texas was close enough to Kansas to believe that it could be infiltrated by abolitionists, too. A state of paranoia gripped slavers all around the state. They believed that enslaved people and abolitionists were plotting "race wars." This suspicion led to whippings, murders, and church burnings.

[22] Dallas Daily Herald, December 14 1859.

[23] Texas Republican (Marshall, TX), November 12 1859.

the "frontier" between Anglo and Native American civilizations, and only a few would-be farmers lived west of Gainesville. The majority of white people who migrated to Cooke County tended to come from the north-ward inland states, such as Arkansas, Tennessee, Ohio, Indiana, and Missouri. They were not slavers but yeoman farmers who sought to grow crops and trade with the Chickasaws across the Red River, the main trading item at this point being bison hides. This did not mean that they were abolitionists, just that they did not have a stake in the Civil War. Those who had a stake in the Civil War — to protect slavery — were small in number but held a disproportionate amount of power in the county.

Several Chickasaw families in Pickens County (today's Love County) owned people. Chickasaws from prominent families like the Colberts and Loves had assimilated to white Southern culture in their homelands of Kentucky and later, Alabama and Mississippi. There, they cultivated cotton and forced African Americans to work the fields. The Chickasaw planter families were partially white, with Anglo men having married Chickasaw women. They attended either Presbyterian or Baptist churches, dressed in western fashion, sent their children to nearby boarding schools, spoke Chickasaw, and ate traditional Chickasaw foods.[24] Their ties to southern secessionists caused both animosity and approval from full-blood Chickasaws. Full-blooded Chickasaws viewed the Democrat Party as the instigator of their removals, but they also distrusted and disliked the U.S. government and military, which supported and enforced the removals. Still other full-blood Chickasaws recognized the precarious position that

---

[24] Full-blood Chickasaws were not as prosperous and not as assimilated into the dominant culture as those from mixed-ethnic backgrounds.

secessionists had created for the Chickasaw tribe and viewed defection from the United States as catastrophic for the future of their nation. The Civil War did not bode well for them.

None of the people and families who would later make up the patchwork of owners of the Stark Ranch lived in Cooke County at the time of the Civil War. However, while the conflict left this tract of the Red River physically untouched, the reverberations of the sectional violence in this period are still felt throughout the county, due in particular to the "Great Hanging of Gainesville" that left over thirty men dead.

Gainesville Hanging

In 1860, James Bourland and William Young comprised the two largest slave-owners in the county. Both men were well acquainted with each other, too. Both William Young and James Bourland to Texas from Tennessee in the 1830s, settled the Red River in today's Lamar and Red River counties, and traded in human beings and livestock. They both dabbled in politics, led raids against Native Americans, and served in the Mexican-American War (1846-1848). After the war, the men claimed several land grants throughout Grayson and Cooke counties. "Claiming land" was a simple process in this period; all white men had to do was stake the land and file a preemption certificate with the Texas General Land Office. The premise of preemption is based on the ability to improve the land. Since Bourland and Young were both slave-owners, they were able to establish cattle and farm operations on their claimed land by using this labor pool, and they quickly became the largest capitalists in the western Red River Valley. They used their economic advantages to take control of the county, leading Indian patrols and county government.

> There is great excitement in Gainesville Texas (according to rebel accounts), owing to the discovery of a secret organization of Lincolnites, the object of which was to destroy all secessionists and take movable plunder to Missouri, and burn what might be left. Five hundred militia collected and caught 20 Lincolnites, and hung two of them.

11. The "excitement" against abolitionists, called Lincolnites, in Cooke County led to mob executions (Cleveland Morning Leader (OH), November 1862, Newspapers.com).

As the Civil War (1861-1865) proved long and arduous, Texas instituted the Confederate Conscription Act in 1862, but this draft was not universal. Wealthy men could hire substitutes to fight in their stead, and railroad workers, teachers, doctors, and clergy members were exempted. Slave owners could be exempted, too, as the "Twenty Negro Law" allowed large scale slave-holders to bypass military service. Thirty non-slaveholding men from Cooke County signed a petition against the law and formed several Union Leagues to counteract the Confederate powerbrokers in the region, which led to retaliation from Bourland and Young. After arresting over one hundred and fifty men in October, Bourland and Young hastily set up a court in Gainesville, mainly composed of slave-owning jurors, who convicted several Union League members for treason. After a mob lynched fourteen of the convicted men, Young and another man were killed out of revenge, which prompted the trial and execution of nineteen more men. The hangings of the convicted men took place along the banks of Pecan Creek, a stream that originates at Stark Ranch, just to the east of the town square. This violence was not isolated to Cooke County; hangings of anti-draft protestors also occurred in Grayson, Wise, and Denton counties. For years afterward, the counties experienced revenge killings between the families of the slain men and those responsible for the "Great Hangings." None of the men who murdered the Unionists for opposing the draft ever faced criminal charges, and the Texas government actively applauded their actions.

Frontier Murders

The murders cast a pall on Cooke County's history, and they constituted part of other violent incidents in the volatile late 19th and early 20th centuries. In October of 1863, four members of the Porter family were killed on Mountain Creek in western Cooke County during a Comanche raid. In retaliation, Cooke County militia battled over one hundred Comanches at South Fish Creek the following December, where fighters on both sides were killed. A party composed of one hundred and twenty five Native Americans, tribe unknown, plundered farms at the edge of Cooke and Denton counties in 1866.[25] In 1868, over three hundred Kiowas and Comanches, led by Chief Big Tree, raided farms and murdered at least twelve settlers at the border of Cooke and Montague counties.[26] An editorial blurb in *The Texas Republican* from December of 1868 argued that Cooke, Wise and Denton counties "have been nearly depopulated" by the "perilous condition" of the frontier and

---

[25] Dallas Daily Herald, October 6 1866.
[26] The Comanche raids of 1863 and the Big Tree raid of 1868 are mapped and detailed in the online encyclopedia Border Land: The Struggle for Texas, 1820-1879. This online tool is published by the University of Texas – Arlington.

warned that "unless relief is afforded these counties will have to be abandoned to the savages."[27]

Hope

While the violence in Cooke County seemed to spell doom and gloom, not all hope was lost. Apparently, despite these raids and the dramatic observation that Cooke County might flounder, an unfounded rumor appeared in 1869: that a railroad was coming to Gainesville. In a letter to the *Dallas Daily Herald* editor, William Thomas Green Weaver, a lawyer and a poet, boasted that Gainesville, in spite that "fearful Indian raids have depopulated our western border," had been selected to be "the half-way station between Kansas City and the Gulf." Gainesville, Weaver explained, would become "the Emporium of Texas" as the railroad would boost Cooke County's fortunes.[28]

Weaver alluded to the Houston and Texas Central Railway, but this railroad never entered Gainesville; it instead snaked from Houston into Dallas, Sherman, and Denison.[29] And, well into the 1880s, Gainesville continued to lack a good road, whether one made of iron or dirt, that led straight north into

---

[27] The Texas Republican (Marshall, TX), December 18 1868.
[28] Dallas Daily Herald, February 6 1869. Weaver, originally from Tennessee, died in Gainesville in 1876 from a drug overdose.
[29] In 1873, the Houston and Texas Central Railway (H&TC) established its own town, Red River City, to compete with Denison, which had been established by the Missouri, Kansas and Texas Railway (MKT) in 1872. The H&TC purposefully bypassed Denison as a snub to the MKT. The railroads had agreed to meet at the Red River, but the MKT had laid tracks south of the river to claim a stake in Texas instead. However, Red River City, which was situated directly at Colbert's Ferry at a Shawnee village and along the Butterfield Overland Stagecoach crossing, was ultimately an unsuccessful settlement.

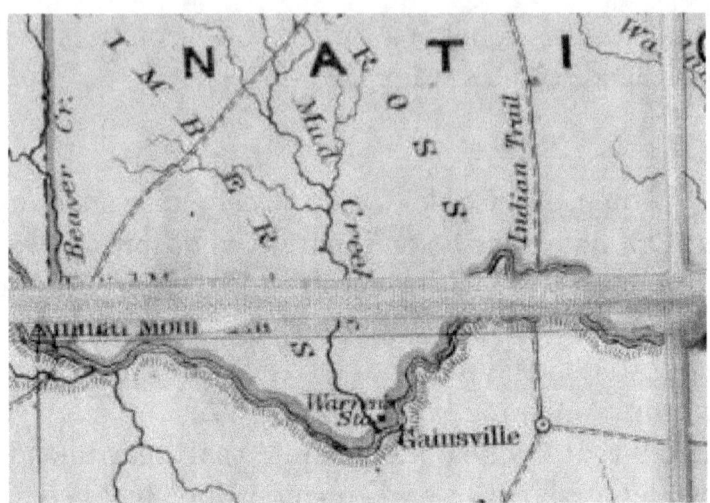

12. *This 1866 military map shows Gainesville connected to an "Indian Trail" that was also called "Whiskey Trail" by locals. The faulty contours of the Red River on this map indicate that the middle section of the Red River remained largely unsurveyed at this time (Library of Congress).*

Indian Territory. Any traveler who wanted to visit Gainesville entered Cooke County from the east or west — one such road was blazed by Henry O. Flipper, the first black graduate of West Point, who surveyed a road between Gainesville and Fort Sill via Clay County in the 1870s.[30] Only a foot path, labeled an "Indian Trail" in a U.S. military map from 1866 and used by Texans to peddle illicit whiskey and by Chickasaws to sell bison hides, linked Gainesville straight north via a ford to the west of Stark Ranch. This is possibly a result of the dense Cross Timbers forest that surrounded the river for miles north and south at the deep bend; this land could seem forbidding, dark, and dangerous. But this all changed in the 1870s, when the land that encompassed the Stark Ranch found some enterprising new owners.

---

[30] Theodore D. Harris, "Flipper, Henry Ossian." *The Encyclopedia of Oklahoma History and Culture.*

Chapter 3
Over the River

Traditional histories have maintained the myth that Reconstruction (1866-1877) undermined the Texas economy, but the historical reality has proved these assertions wrong. The influx of northern "carpetbagger" money directly boosted Gainesville's fortunes, and while Reconstruction brought social upheaval, it carried an economic boom that had its beginnings in 1866.

The Cattle
Immediately after the Civil War, several large ranches organized in southern Indian Territory across from Cooke County. The bison hunts of the mid 1860s in the prairies of Cooke and Pickens counties made way for larger cattle holdings, and while the war had put a damper on the trade, it quickly reinvigorated after the war ended. The ranchers were mainly Anglo men who eagerly bought Texas cattle and sold bison hides in Texas. R. L. Nichols, who lived in Gainesville in

1874, recalled that "one business that helped to keep Gainesville going was the 'hide trains' that passed through there on their way to Jefferson, Texas… it was a great sight to see from twenty-five to fifty ox teams of ten yoke hitched to a big wagon to which would be two trail wagons attached and all loaded with buffalo hides."[31]

13. Ranch in Cooke County (Morton Museum).

Cattle management, whether on the hoof or in the pasture, remained the chief economic engine in the Red River Valley surrounding Cooke County. This became especially true after 1866, when the Grant administration forced the Chickasaw Nation to release the western half of its lands to form the Kiowa, Apache and Comanche Reservation; Anglos like Isaac Cloud founded ad-hoc ranches and blazed trails to supply beef to the tribes and the forts, making large fortunes on government contracts.[32] By the 1880s, Texas cattle grazed on

---

[31] Indian Pioneer Papers, "R. L. Nichols," (1937).

[32] Isaac Cloud was from Alabama but followed the Chickasaws from their Mississippi homelands into Indian Territory in order to supply this ready-made customer base with beef before and after the Civil War. Because he was not a Chickasaw, he had no rights to land in Indian Territory. His brother, however, married a Chickasaw woman and her heritage granted the Cloud family access to the land and tribal government. Cloud thus

both sides of the river in large numbers. According to Chickasaw law, Texans had to pay grazing fees per head of cattle, which was difficult to calculate and collect on the open range. Periodically, the Chickasaw Nation sent militia to herd cattle back across the Red River into Texas, but the Texan ranchers simply moved their herds back into the territory without consequence.[33] By 1898, the Curtis Act passed that allowed farmers and citizens to confiscate cattle and demand to payment for grazing.[34]

Throughout the latter half of the 1860s and beyond, Anglo settlers came to Gainesville in droves, arriving on foot or by covered wagon via fords or crossing the river on the ferries at Colbert, Preston, and Burneyville. Many also came from the interior of Texas, seeking economic opportunities in the Red River border region. Some of this population influx was temporary, a result of the cattle drives that took beeves along trails that stretched from South Texas and Mexico to the new railhead at Abilene, Kansas. One of these paths is now known as the Chisholm Trail.

Cattle Trail

The term "Chisholm Trail" actually never applied to Texas. Cowboys and ranchers used the term in the 20th century to describe the work they did to newspapers and WPA

---

founded a "ranch" on land he simply used and improved but did not hold title to. He blazed a trail from the ranch near today's Leon to Gainesville, which ultimately connected Gainesville to Chickasha.

[33] Indian Pioneer Papers, "R. L. Nichols," (1937)

[34] Curtis Act, 30 Stat. 495, c.517: "An Act for the Protection of the Indian Territory and for Other Purposes." In 1902, Texas cattlemen sued the Chickasaw Nation for confiscating their cattle under this act. The lawsuit, Morris v. Hitchcock (1904) found its way to the Supreme Court, where the judges ruled in favor of the Chickasaw Nation's land rights.

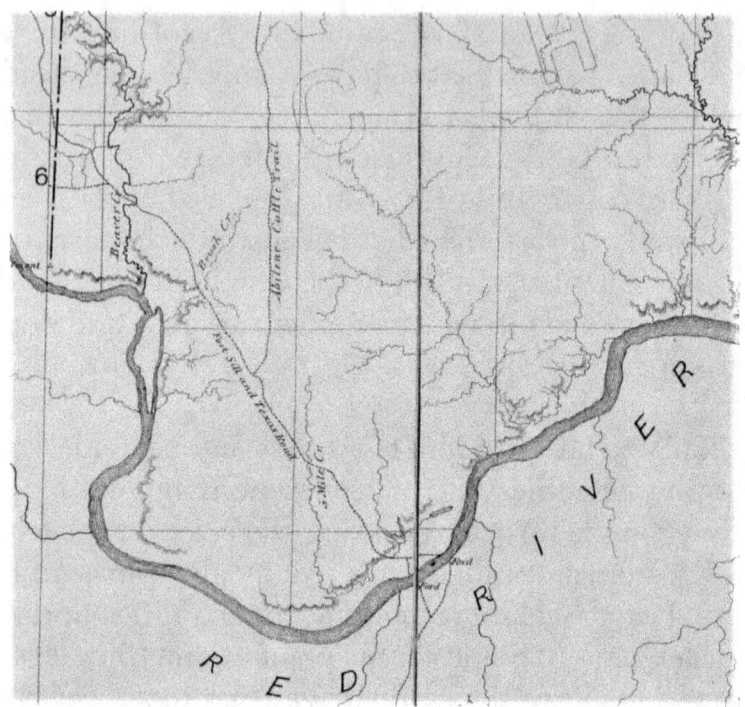

14. *The 1872 military map of the Chickasaw Nation was one of the first geographically accurate maps of the middle Red River Valley. It places the Abilene Cattle Trail, known colloquially as the "Chisholm Trail," in today's Jefferson County, Oklahoma, which is north of Montague County, Texas (Library of Congress).*

interviewers; saying "going up the Chisholm Trail" became a short-hand way of detailing the work cattle drivers engaged in. The named path was given disproportionate significance when automobile tourism in the 1920s promoted the romantic scenery associated with cattle driving by assigning various unnamed beef trails the moniker, "Chisholm Trail." The actual Chisholm Trail existed only in Kansas and northern Indian Territory, and was labeled as the "Abilene Trail" on contemporary maps and as the "McCoy Trail" in newspapers. In 1866, Joseph McCoy, a cattle dealer from Illinois, worked with the nascent dugout town of Abilene, Kansas to entice a railroad to terminate there. McCoy and his associates built a stockyard at the terminus and surveyed a trail that led southward from Abilene to the Canadian River near Jesse Chisholm's supply store. Then, McCoy promoted Abilene as the best and safest place for Texas cattlemen to sell and ship their beeves as the pre-Civil War Shawnee Trail (also known as the Texas Cattle Road) had become populated by squatters, farmers, and emigrants. Texans agreed and soon engaged in the booming cattle drives.

In Cooke County, the cattle crossings were at Walnut Bend, Sivell's Bend, or at the ford used by the Cloud Ranch. The main trail crossing was at Red River Station in Montague County, where the Texas state government collected revenues and cattle were treated against the tick that carried the dreaded "Texas fever."[35] Although Gainesville was not on a main path, the town benefitted greatly from the cattle going up the various trails. Merchants eagerly outfitted the drives with supplies, especially saddles, and Gainesville also became a center of trade for the stockmen who sold cattle to the ranches, reservations, and military installations in Indian Territory.

Gainesville's prosperity allowed the city to incorporate in 1873. Yet by 1875 still, no decent northern road existed to link Gainesville to Indian Territory, let alone a ferry crossing. This changed when two ferries were established less than a mile from each other at the deep Red River bend between Cooke

---

[35] Longhorn cattle were immune from the effects of a tickborne disease that became known as "Texas fever," but other cattle breeds were not. The state of Kansas prohibited the importation of Longhorn cattle due danger posed to its livestock industry. Most drovers ignored the ban and instead relied on quarantines and dipping vats at border crossings like Red River Station, Montague County, Texas.

Stark Ranch of Cooke County, Texas: History that spans the Red River

and Pickens (Love) counties. These ferries formed the nucleus of Stark Ranch.

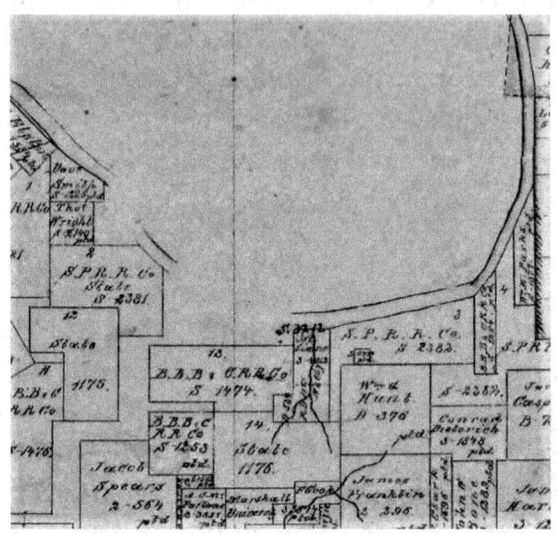

15. *The land surrounding the deep bend of the Red River in Cooke County was reserved for railroad investment; the railroads never used the land to raise capital (1868, Texas General Land Office).*

Free Land

Cooke County emerged from the Peter's Colony Land Grant Company, an empresario scheme established during the Republic of Texas (1836-1845) that encompassed much of the Red River Valley. Agents for the colony received portions of each land grant taken; in exchange, the agents surveyed the land, deeded the title, and provided seed and supplies to settlers. The maximum land grants were 640 acres for a family and 320 acres for single men. The success of Peter's Colony depended on the hostilities between white settlers and native tribes. Settlers in Denton, Dallas, and Collin counties benefitted the most due to the peace treaty signed at Bird's Fort (1843), which was negotiated between Edward H. Tarrant, George W. Terrell, and the Wichita tribes. Settlers in

Cooke County, however, continued to experience raids. Additionally, parts of the counties under the empresario scheme had already been pre-empted, which complicated legal matters. The result was that not many farms and homesteads in Cooke County derived from the land grant, as newcomers continued to squat rather than follow the law.

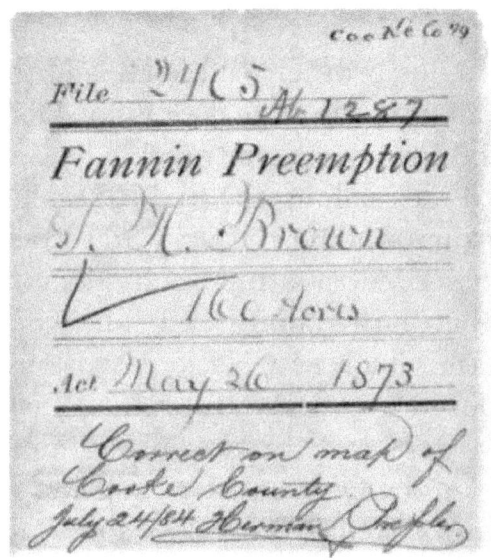

16. S.H. Brown's preemption certificate, filed in 1873 (Texas General Land Office).

After the Civil War, unclaimed sections of land throughout the state were set aside for railroad companies and public schools in the hopes of raising funds for their construction. In Cooke County, the state deeded large tracts of these "unassigned lands" to the Buffalo Bayou, Brazos and Colorado Railway at the deep bend of the Red River. The railroad company never did anything with the land, however. Instead, Samuel H. Brown and L. M. Ford filed pre-emption certificates in 1873 and 1879, respectively, on 160 acres each — the largest amount of land qualified for pre-emption after 1866 — upon notification of improvements they had made on the land.[36] Ford's pre-emption was challenged by R. W. Taylor in 1883, who claimed that he had made the improvements, and Ford quit claimed the pre-emption certificate to Taylor for $100. Brown retained title to his land and established the first ferry that connected Gainesville directly to Indian Territory.

Brown's Ferry

Samuel H. Brown, his brother, Alfred R., and their employee, Will Smith, began operating the eponymous ferry sometime in 1876 or 1877, and Brown's Ferry quickly became one of the more popular crossings along the Red River. The Browns farmed the land surrounding the ferry and worked as carpenters when needed, creating a self-sustaining operation that supported their large family well. They also farmed and ranched land in the Chickasaw Nation across from their Texas ferry site after purchasing leases from the Washington and McKish ranches. One of the Browns brought examples of their cotton harvest into the Gainesville newspaper offices to boast of the richness in the Red River Valley soil.[37] The Browns lent their name to the freshwater spring on the north bank of the Red River; the *Oklahoma Daily Register* mentions J. C. Brown, another relation to the Brown brothers, operating the ferry at the spring.[38] Jennie Selfridge, a WPA field worker, described the spring as "an abundant supply of water, which forms a large pool near the north bank of Red River."[39]

---

[36] Texas General Land Office, Fannin scrip, Brown & Taylor; Texas General Land Office, "Categories of Land Grants."
[37] Gainesville Daily Hesperian, September 3, 1888.
[38] Oklahoma History Center
[39] Indian Pioneer Papers, "Jennie Selfridge, Brown Spring," October 1937.

17. The ferry at Warren's Bend, pictured here, was similar in design to Brown's Ferry (Morton Museum).

The Brown family was originally from Collin County and came to Cooke County in 1874. Samuel Brown had served in the Confederate Army. In 1888, he left the ferry operation to find a new fortune in Oklahoma Territory, where he established "the largest farm in the Chickasaw Nation" comprising four thousand acres west of Ardmore.[40] Alfred Brown operated the ferry for most of his life and his obituary referred to him as "Grandpa Brown… a good man, of upright demeanor and sterling character."[41]

At first, Brown used poles to propel the ferry forward, but as demand for the ferry increased, the Brown brothers suspended cables across the river to pull the ferry across.[42] Brown's Ferry became a sought-after crossing point. Already in 1876, the *Gainesville Hesperian* described the ferry as an "institution" in a tongue-in-cheek account: "It has been established but a short time, and been kept busy during the time. The amount of

---

[40] "Samuel A. Brown." www.rootsweb.ancestry.com
[41] Dallas News, March 17 1921.
[42] Indian Pioneer papers, "W.R. Mulkey," (1937).

crossings for the first month were 400 men, 50 women, 150 children, 200 wagons, 1 bunch and buggy, 450 horses and mules, 80 sheep, 150 head of cattle, 4000 [sic] bushels of corn, 200 bushels of wheat, 5000 [sic] pounds of bacon, 25 hogs, 500 dogs and 25 deadbeats."[43] Brown's ferry also provided entertainment of sorts: in 1894, "several of Gainesville's Terpsichorean artists" danced on the "ferry-boat which was launched on the turbulent waters of the Red River."[44]

Recognizing the need for a continuous crossing, the Texas senate passed a bill sponsored by Senator Coke in 1886 to authorize the Chickasaw Bridge Company to build a bridge "at or near Brown's Ferry" which became law in 1887; however, no bridge was built at this time.[45] Apparently anticipating a bridge that wouldn't materialize until the 1930s, businessmen along Dye Street (now Weaver Street) in Gainesville founded a subscription to improve the road to Brown's Ferry in 1887.[46]

The Criners
The Criner family from the Chickasaw Nation settled at the spring after the Browns had established the ferry. They founded the small settlement of Criner on the north side of the Red River between the spring and a natural lake that they

---

[43] Galveston Daily News, February 26, 1878.
[44] Daily Hesperian, May 5 1894.
[45] Galveston Daily News, April 29 1886 and Galveston Daily News, March 25, 1887. The same law passed by the 49th congress authorized the Red River Bridge Company, of which William Kilgore was an investor, to build a bridge "across the Red river at or near Denison," most likely at the Colbert's Ferry crossing. Like the one at Brown's Ferry, this bridge was also not built until several decades later.
[46] Fort Worth Daily Gazette, September 4, 1887.

named after themselves, Lake Chriner.[47] The Criners also established a family cemetery in a hill above the spring, which is now known as the Brown's Spring Cemetery. Some members of the Love family, prominent Chickasaws whose name now graces the former Pickens County, are buried at the Brown's Spring Cemetery as the families had intermarried. The Criners also helped to establish Thackerville a few miles distant from Brown Springs. During the allotment period of

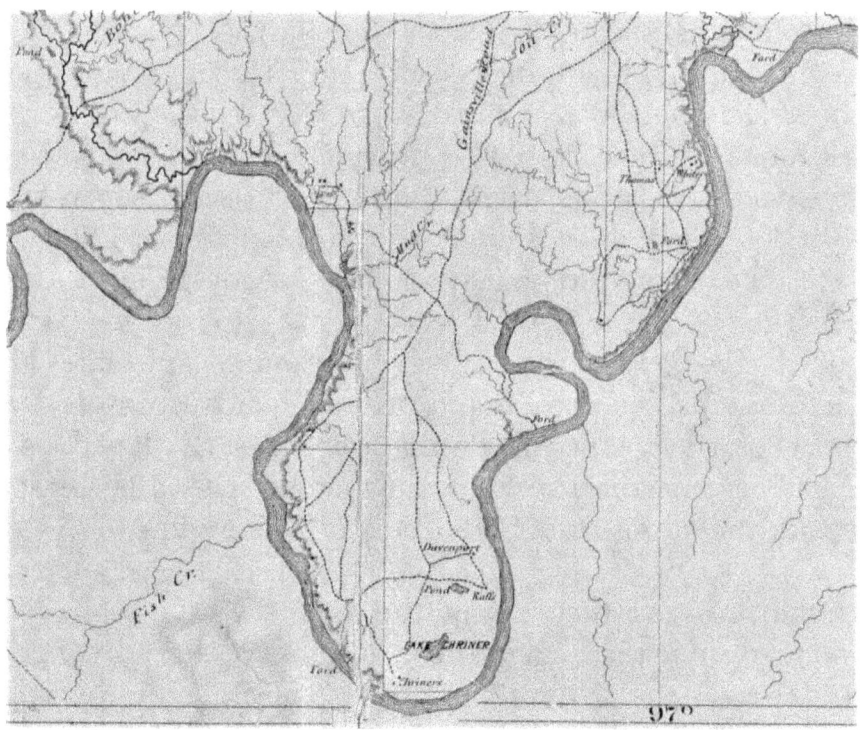

18. *The Criners settled around a natural lake at the deep bend near Brown's Spring. Military mapmakers misspelled their last name as "Chriner" when they labeled the lake (1872, Library of Congress).*

---

[47] The family name, Criner, is recorded on the Dawes Rolls, census, and in other official documents. However, an 1866 map of Indian Territory misspelled Criner as Chriner, and subsequent maps continued to print the misspelling.

1903, the Criners gained individual title to land,[48] but their land allotments were not situated at Brown's Spring. Instead, their allotments became known as the "Criner Hills," a world-famous geological and paleontological site due to the discovery of ancient rock formations and fossil beds between today's Love and Carter counties, Oklahoma.

The land that the Criners first settled upon at Brown's Spring was eventually deeded to J. D. Leeper, a merchant from Texas who co-founded the Scott-Leeper Company, a department store in Madill. In fact, Leeper and John Mahan bought most of the land along the deep bend of the Red River opposite of Stark Ranch in the early 20th century, including Lake Chriner, from Choctaw and Chickasaw allotments.[49] J. D. Leeper; his bother, J. G.; and J. C. Graham incorporated Leeper Lake in 1918.[50] The partners renamed the lake to Moutry Duck Lake, but by the 1950s, the United States Geological Survey had begun to label it Leeper Lake.[51] Leeper and his associates kept the lake as a private retreat and sued against trespassers, even those who collected pecans on the properties. By the 1950s, the lake had become a private resort owned by several business interests, including First State Bank of Gainesville.

Both the Criner settlement and the cemetery have been abandoned since the turn of the 20th century, but remnants of their existence are still visible. Brown's Spring still flows unencumbered, and until the mid-20th century, the spring was promoted in the WPA Guide of Oklahoma as a road trip

---

[48] Chickasaw Indian Rolls #1790
[49] Oral history of John Mahan from Leeper Lake, 1944.
[50] Enid Daily Eagle, June 10, 1918.
[51] Love County records; Marietta Monitor, October 8 1915.

destination.⁵² A sunken trace exists that takes visitors to the cemetery at the top of the hill. Lake Chriner/ Moutry Duck Lake/ Leeper Lake is still a privately owned fishing retreat.

Foreigners in the Territory
Brown's Ferry served travelers and settlers coming into Texas, but also became a conduit for an Anglo invasion into Indian Territory. Prior to the allotment divisions instigated by the Dawes Severalty Act of 1887, the Chickasaws saw the land as communal property.⁵³ Chickasaw families who held greater wealth and connections were often intermarried with Anglos, but they, too, simply set up farms, ranches, ferries, and plantations through improvements, not by deeds and legal transactions. However, men who belonged to the tribe gained voting rights, even if their association was through marriage and not blood. With all this free range and fertile soil, land-hungry Texans who had no connection to the Chickasaws still sought access to the territory.

> PERMIT LAW OF THE CHICKASAW NATION.
> SECTION 1. Be it enacted by the legislature of the Chickasaw Nation, That citizens of any State or Territory of the United States wishing to hire or rent land, or be otherwise employed in this nation, shall be required to enter into contract with a citizen; said contract to be reported by the citizen to the county clerk of the county where said citizen resides.

19. The 1876 permit law required all non-Chickasaws to pay a fee and enter into a contract with Chickasaw citizens if they wanted to rent land (University of Oklahoma).

At first, the Chickasaw Nation allowed non-Chickasaws, whom they deemed "foreigners," range and employment rights in exchange for a $5 permit fee. As more and more Anglos entered the territory, Governor Benjamin Overton raised the

---
⁵² WPA Guide to Oklahoma, 1986.
⁵³ Dawes Act, 1889.

annual fee in 1876 and increased its militia to ferret out non-permit holders.[54] Brown's Ferry took the Texan hopefuls across the river into the Chickasaw Nation, but the ferry also transported the squatters back to Texas. Lillie Sprowls, an Anglo Texan whose family had come to the Chickasaw Nation at Brown's Spring in 1875, told a WPA interviewer in 1937 that when the Chickasaws raised the permit fee "to twenty-five dollars and some of the people would not pay it, the militia would come over and put the people who would not pay over on the Texas side. These people got tired of being moved so one time when the militia had put a crowd of people over on the Texas side… the people who had been put over into Texas began to shoot in the air above the heads of the militia."[55] While the U.S. Senate upheld the rights of the Chickasaws to issue permits and restrict immigration into its nation, Texans continued to flock into the territory and often, actively undermined the act's enforcements. Lille Sprowls remembered that her mother hid a Texas man in her home from the militia, which Sprowls explained was "to protect this man."[56]

Sacra's Ferry
Brown's Ferry was not the only transport across the Red River at the deep bend. Ed Sacra obtained the portion of land along the Red River that had first been issued to L. M. Ford as Fannin Scrip, who then quit-claimed to R. W. Taylor when he demonstrated that he, and not Ford, had improved the land. Since the Sacras grazed cattle on both sides of the river, they built a ferry for their own purposes which they allowed the public to access. But in 1887, T. M. King took over the ferry operation when Ed Sacra did not pay the taxes. The deed

---
[54] Permit Law of the Chickasaw Nation, 1876.
[55] Indian Pioneer Papers, "Lillie Sprowls," 1937.
[56] Ibid

described the mortgaged property as "a certain ferry boat and wire cable across Red River known as Sacra Ferry and things pertaining to said Ferry boat also one ... house with two rooms."[57] The city of Gainesville opened Grand Avenue, its first improved road, to Sacra's Ferry in October of 1887.[58]

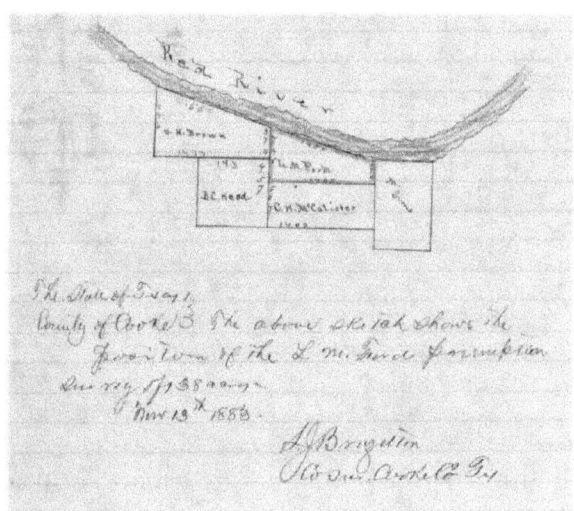

20. *The Sacra brothers obtained part of the Ford preemption in the 1880s (Texas General Land Office).*

The Sacra brothers — Ed, Richard, and James — were Anglos from Grayson County. Ed Sacra had married Mattie Carter, a woman with Chickasaw heritage, and they had several children together. Mattie was the widow to Benjamin Overton, the prominent governor of the Chickasaw Nation, and had at least two children with him who made it to adulthood. These family ties gave the Sacra brothers access to the Chickasaw lands in addition to owning their own land in Cooke County. They

---

[57] Cooke County Deed Records. Deed of Trust 005 (1887): T.M. King to H. Hulen trustee for Ed Sacra. Harvey Hulen was a surveyor and the Cooke County tax collector (Texas Bonds and Oaths of Office, 1846-1920, 1880).
[58] Fort Worth Daily Gazette, September 14 1887.

became successful cattle ranchers and shared the land, at least sometimes... because the borderland that their lives, ferries, and ranches straddled was often fraught with violence.

21. Ed Sacra married Chickasaw Governor's widow, Mattie Overton, and therefore gained access to Chickasaw lands (National Archives).

Borderlands

The Red River has always been a significant boundary in American history. Before 1798, it was point of contention between the French and Spanish empires. After 1803, the river became the border between the United States and New Spain, which was solidified in the Adams-Onis Treaty of 1819. By 1821, it divided the United States and Mexico and after 1836, the United States and the Republic of Texas. Beyond Texas statehood, the river remained a boundary between Anglo-centric Texas and the nations of Indian Territory. Even today, the line between Texas and Oklahoma is a fine one. The river doesn't like to be confined to its borders and is ever-changing, often leading to human instability.

This volatility was first experienced with the natural environment in the region. The Red River Valley at the deep bend once teemed with prairie chickens, wild pigeons, wild cattle, wild burros and wild horses. Bison were plentiful, but this abundance quickly ended: "It was a great slaughter as thousands and thousands of buffaloes were slain," R. L. Nichols related. "The hides had been skinned from buffaloes that were being killed on the west Texas plains by hunters who killed for the hides only." The slaughter left behind millions of bones, which generated a booming bone-hauling business. Traders on ox carts laden with bison bones came to Gainesville throughout the 1870s to sell them as fertilizer. By the turn of the 20th century, the bison, chickens, and pigeons were gone from the prairie, replaced by wild pigs and wild horses. The wild horses, however, did not adapt well to barbed wire, which made its debut on the open range in the deep bend area in the 1880s. R. L. Nichols explained that they would get entangled in the barbed wire and kill themselves in their panic.[59]

The lawlessness of the border region, where those escaping from the law on either side could simply cross the Red River and evade consequences, reared its head often. Cattle, hog and horse thieves were arrested at both the Sacra and Brown ferries, which the sheriff of Cooke County and the militia from the Indian Territory monitored for just such occurrences.[60] Dead and injured men were sometimes found on the Brown Ferry and Sacra Ferry roads.[61] Cowboys from the Chickasaw Nation ranches enjoyed partying in Gainesville and harassing local law enforcement, and although the road between Gainesville and Brown's Ferry was well-traveled, the citizens and businesses used a site "within 300 hundred yards of the public road leading to Brown's ferry" as a dead animal

---

[59] Indian Pioneer Papers. "R. L. Nichols," (1937).
[60] Gainesville Daily Hesperian, April 6 1897; Gainesville Daily Hesperian, September 25 1889; Gainesville Daily Hesperian, January 30 1889; Daily Ardmoreite, July 11 1895.
[61] Fort Worth Daily Gazette, November 5 1886; Daily Ardmoreite, September 14 1913.

dumping ground.[62] The dangers of the river brought more than a few travelers to their watery graves, too.[63] A flashflood almost killed Alfred Brown and Will Smith when the cable holding the ferry broke in the swift current.[64]

22. *The Brown and Ford preemptions laid the groundwork for the Stark Ranch (1899, Texas General Land Office).*

Tragedy struck the Brown and Sacra families, too. In 1889, Alfred Brown, the twenty-five year old son of the ferry operator who had recently married a fourteen year old girl from Dallas, died inside his parents' home at Brown's Ferry after suffering a gunshot leveled by Will Stone from Thackerville.[65] Tom Brown, once the operator of the ferry, was stabbed to death by an acquaintance on Halloween night

---

[62] Gainesville Daily Hesperian, May 8 1888.
[63] Gainesville Daily Hesperian, May 15 1888; Daily Ardmoreite, March 21 1894; Fort Worth Daily Gazette, September 12 1886.
[64] Fort Worth Daily Gazette, June 26 1885.
[65] Gainesville Daily Hesperian, May 1 1889.

of 1916, his body found alone in his cabin near the Red River.[66] The Browns sold the ferry and the eighty acres surrounding it to A. C. and Hettie Rose in 1899. The family moved to Davis in the Chickasaw Nation, where Alfred Senior, the original ferry operator, died in 1921.[67]

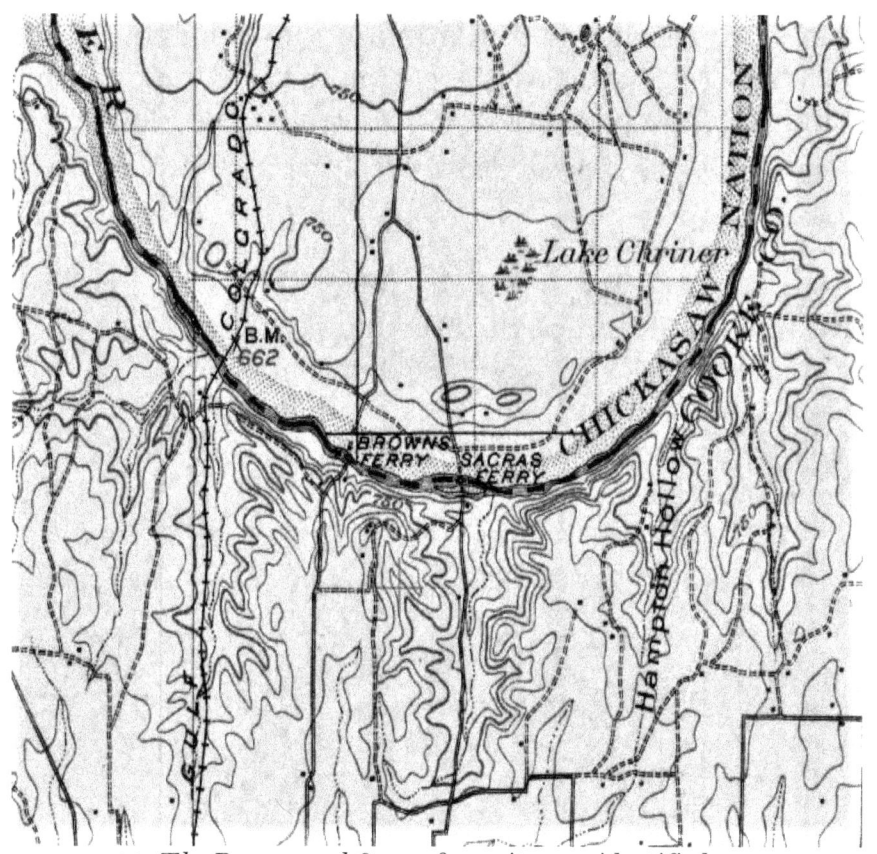

23. *The Brown and Sacra ferry sites are identified on a geologic map from 1902 (U.S. Geological Survey).*

---

[66] Ron Melugin, *Heroes, Scoundrels and Angels: Fairview Cemetery of Gainesville, Texas*, 2010.
[67] Davis News (Davis, OK), March 17 1921.

James Sacra was shot in 1888 by his own relation. He scuffled with his brother Ed's stepson, Charles Overton (grandson of Benjamin Overton, Governor of the Chickasaw Nation) over cattle that had wandered onto Richard Sacra's pasture at Oakland near Pottsboro in Grayson County.[68] Overton claimed self-defense but still faced a grand jury. Richard Sacra, brother of James, died in the Ardmore Sanitorium in 1910 after a short coma. The attending doctor noted that "he had the appearance… of a man who had been administered a drug," but no inquiry was made into his death.[69]

The economic boom of the 1880s may have played a role in the violence that occurred at or near the ferries, because this decade witnessed Gainesville becoming connected by two railroads. While the city and the county prospered, the social upheaval generated from the construction of the railways literally, figuratively, and permanently changed the Red River Valley's landscape.

---

[68] Fort Worth Daily Gazette, December 18 1888.
[69] Daily Ardmoreite, September 9 1910.

Chapter 4
Connecting the River

Texas and Indian Territory entered the industrial age after the Civil War, when fates and fortunes became tied to the railroads that had finally made their appearance in the state and territory. Prior to 1865 in Texas, only about eighty miles of track had been laid by the Buffalo Bayou, Brazos and Colorado Railway. As the first railroad charter in Texas, high hopes were pinned on this operation, but it went bankrupt after 1865 and eventually came under the umbrella of the Houston and Texas Central Railway. Likewise, investors in the Texas Western Railroad Company had run track between Longview and Waskom by 1860, and the company had hoped to extend the North Louisiana and Texas Railroad Company from Shreveport to Marshall. This plan wasn't realized until 1872, when the Texas and Pacific Railway acquired these tracks and began building to Dallas.

The MKT

As a federal territory, the nations in the Indian Territory could not procure their own charters. Instead, the federal government gave an exclusive contract to the Union Pacific, Southern Branch to construct a line from Missouri to the Texas border after the railroad had won a competition between two other railroad companies when it was the first to enter Indian Territory from the north. In 1870, the railroad had changed its name to the Missouri, Kansas and Texas Railway (MKT) and did not just build a railroad bed in Indian Territory; it also funded coal mining operations in the Choctaw Nation.[70]

By late 1872, the MKT built the first railroad bridge across the river between Texas and Indian Territory, arriving at the Red River near Colbert's Ferry, Chickasaw Nation, Indian Territory before Christmas. While the state of Texas had a decided interest in the MKT and its connection to St. Louis and Chicago, the MKT had not been chartered in Texas and technically, was not supposed to breach the southern bank of the Red River, but it did so, anyway. The company laid another ten miles of track into Grayson County, where it founded the terminus town of Denison on Christmas Day, 1872. By this time, the Houston and Texas Central Railway had been building northward from Sherman and bypassed Denison in favor of its own terminus town. The railroad founded Red River City (formerly Shawneetown) at the base of the MKT bridge in early 1873. Since the two lines did not connect, interstate travel remained difficult until the Houston and Texas Central Railway established its own depot in Denison in late 1873.

---

[70] Jack Maguire, *Katy's Baby: The Story of Denison, Texas*, 1991.

24. *The MKT bridge over the Red River between Colbert (I.T.) and Denison (TX) in an illustration for Scribener's Monthly (1873, Library of Congress).*

The arrival of a railroad that connected Texas with Chicago heralded an economic boom throughout the Red River Valley, but the financial panic of 1873 retarded further construction. Citizens in Denison did not want their opportunity to languish, however. Denison, which grew practically overnight into a town of thousands after its founding by the MKT, needed connections to the cotton-growing east and the cattle-raising west. By contrast, Gainesville would have to wait for its railroad connection for almost another decade.

The Denison and Pacific
When the MKT's financial struggles disallowed further construction into Texas for the remainder of the 1870s, businessmen in Denison pooled their monies to charter their own railway companies. They founded the Denison and Southeastern Railway Company in 1877, which laid tracks from Denison to Whitewright, Greenville, and eventually, Mineola. In 1878, the businessmen chartered the Denison and Pacific Railway to connect Denison to Whitesboro and

eventually, Gainesville.[71] In late 1879, the first train of the Denison and Pacific Railway reached Gainesville laden with flour.[72] The county seat of the old "frontier" finally entered the railroad age: the Denison and Pacific Railway connected Gainesville to Dallas and Fort Worth via Whitesboro and connected Gainesville to Chicago and the Gulf of Mexico via Denison.

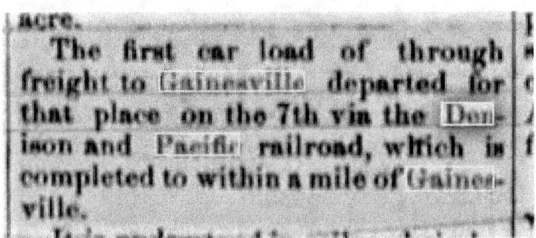

25. *The first train bound for Gainesville arrived in November 1879 (The Marshall Messenger, Newspapers.com).*

The Denison and Pacific Railway's charter explicitly stated that the railroad was to be built to Fort Belknap in Young County, which at this point still an important telegraph relay station. However, the company could not successfully secure more funding. In 1880, the Missouri, Kansas and Texas Railway acquired the Denison and Pacific Railway. In 1887, the MKT bought the tracks of the Gainesville, Henrietta and Western Railway Company after it had completed seventy miles of track from Gainesville to Henrietta. Thus, in 1887, Gainesville enjoyed an east-west through connection on the rail, paralleling the direction of Gainesville's stagecoach and pioneer roads. The city and county still lacked an actual thoroughfare that ran north/south. This changed the same year.

---

[71] Denison Daily News, December 9 1879.
[72] Galveston Daily News, November 12 1879.

> The people of Denison are very much enthused over its improved railroad prospects. The M., K. and T. company has purchased the Denison Pacific. All trains, etc., in future are to work under M., K. and T. instructions.

26. *The Missouri, Kansas and Texas Railway took over operations of the Denison and Pacific Railway in January of 1880 (The Marshall Messenger, Newspapers.com).*

The Gulf, Colorado and Santa Fe

The Gulf, Colorado and Santa Fe Railway Company (GCSF) was chartered in Texas in 1873 to connect Galveston to Santa Fe, New Mexico. Its topsy-turvy financial problems slowed construction but by the 1880s, it had recovered enough to reach Fort Worth in 1886. In January of that year, J. M. Lindsey and R. S. Rollins from Gainesville successfully courted the GCSF to ensure that the tracks would be laid in Gainesville. The railroad selected a direct route between Fort Worth and Gainesville and bypassed the city of Denton, which had also sent a delegation to the woo the company.[73] Several sections of track began construction simultaneously in Texas and in Indian Territory, in the hopes that the completed right-of-way would be opened to Kansas City in early 1887.

In April of 1886, the GCSF established a camp at the Red River near Brown's Ferry to begin surveying and preparing for the railroad's bridge construction a few hundred yards west

---

[73] Austin American Statesman, January 1886. Caissons are "watertight chambers used in construction work under water or as a foundation." (Merriam Webster). The caissons which had to be poured and set while the water from the river was dammed and pumped away from the riverbed were set "on solid rock twenty-eight feet below the bed of the river." Cullison Banner (Cullison, KS), September 30 1886.

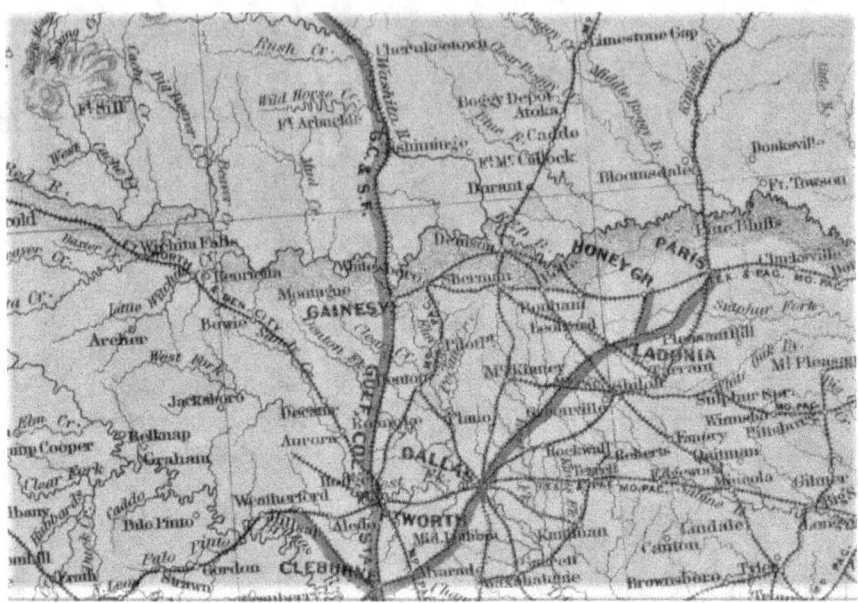
27. Railroads coming into Gainesville by 1888 (UT Arlington).

from the ferry crossing between the land grants once owned by David Smith and J. S. H. Dunham.[74] Masonry work, iron delivery, track grading, and assembly of the bridge took up the rest of the year. The work was delayed slightly due to the Great Southwest Strike. The "force employed on the Santa Fe bridge at Red River sinking caisons" [sic] had demanded higher wages for the dangerous work they were undertaking. Instead, the workers were fired and a new crew from Cincinnati took the strikers' place.[75]

Workmen who laid the ballast, tracks, and constructed the bridge were not locals. Many came from Dallas as general laborers, while masons were brought in from around the

---

[74] David Smith received his patent on 160 acres land in 1859 (00126) and Sallie Donham, wife of J.S.H Donham, received the patent on 160 acres in 1879. (Texas General Land Office).
[75] Fort Worth Daily, Gazette October 20 1886.

United States to build the brick footings for the bridge. The bridge itself was a product of the Phoenix Bridge Company, an iron and steel bridge manufacturer based out of Phoenixville, Pennsylvania.[76] Like other iron works in the late 19th century, the company published a catalog of bridge designs for customers to choose from. The bridge the GCSF selected for the Red River was the same type of bridge constructed over the Washita River near Dougherty (then, Strawberry Flat; the town re-named itself in 1887) in Indian Territory.[77] It boasted "800 feet from end to end, requiring five piers [and] four spans of iron work."[78]

By January of 1887, the bridge was mostly completed, allowing the first train to cross into Indian Territory.[79] An excursion train arrived within a few days, although the bridge was not yet considered safe for passenger crossings. The passengers instead "alighted and walked across Red river on a temporary bridge."[80] Across the river, trains made their first stop in Indian Territory at Thackerville, which was originally one of Pickens County's (now, Love County) earliest settlements. Its founder, Zachariah Thacker from Arkansas, had established a communal farm and grist mill near Watt's Ferry at the Red River after receiving permission from Chickasaw settlers. Upon the GCSF railroad entering Indian Territory, residents removed their homes and businesses in old Thackerville to the tracks to take advantage of the potential wealth that the railroad would bring.

---

[76] Weekly Republican Traveler (Arkansas City, KS), September 4 1886.
[77] Fort Worth Daily Gazette, April 1 1887.
[78] Fort Worth Daily Gazette, January 11 1887.
[79] Fort Worth Daily Gazette, January 9 1887.
[80] Forth Worth Daily Gazette, January 11 1887.

Stark Ranch of Cooke County, Texas: History that spans the Red River

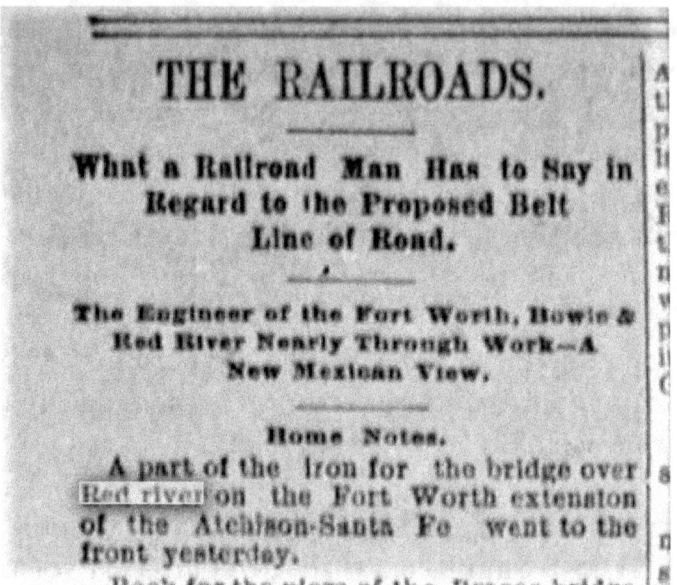

28. *The Fort Worth Daily Gazette monitored the progress of the GCSF daily, and reported on the Red River bridge in detail in 1886 (Newspapers.com).*

The GCSF did not just build tracks and a bridge at Gainesville — it also selected Gainesville for the site of its roundhouse, switching yards, and machine shops. As the city raised $50,000 and purchased fifty acres to entice the railroad company's arrival by the deadline, the GCSF commenced developing Gainesville's industrial landscape in 1887.[81] By the turn of the 20th century, the GCSF replaced most of its wooden buildings in Gainesville with new ones. The bridge across the Red River was replaced around that time, too. Like all of the railroad bridges across the rivers and streams in the Red River Valley, the Santa Fe bridge at Stark Ranch was replaced 1911 due to two reasons: the instability of the structure caused by the

---

[81] ibid

incredible Red River Valley flooding of 1908[82] and a 1906 federal law.

Stark Ranch Begins

Before the 20th century, road bridges across the Red River between Texas and Indian Territory were few in number. In 1875, Benjamin Colbert financed a toll bridge between Colbert (Panola County, Chickasaw Nation, Indian Territory) and Red River City (Grayson County, Texas), built by the National Bridge Company, but it was swept away by floods in 1876 and eventually was replaced by the turn of the 20th century.[83] It was not until a 1906 congressional act authorized the regulation of bridges over rivers and other "navigable waters" that serious bridge building between the territory and state commenced. This act attempted to ensure that bridges, including railroad bridges, met engineering specifications, such as clearance heights to accommodate shipping traffic and functional mechanisms for swing and draw bridges. Further, the law stipulated that railroad and road bridges must accommodate "transmission of the mails, the troops, and munitions of war" as well as "telegraph and telephone lines." Approval of bridge design and construction ultimately rested with the Secretary of War (today, the Secretary of Defense).[84]

---

[82] The 1908 flooding of the Southwest was one of the worst weather events in U.S. history. The upper Red, Canadian, and Arkansas rivers flooded due to sustained rains, which triggered flooding in the Mississippi River. All three forks of the Trinity River and all tributaries for the Red River flooded as well. Almost all railroad bridges had to be replaced throughout southern Oklahoma, northern Texas, and western Arkansas, either due to washouts or severe damage.

[83] Austin American Statesman, September 2 1874 and September 5 1875; Weekly Harald (Marshall, TX), July 11 1876; USGS Map Sherman,1901.

[84] 59th Congress, Session 1, Chapter 1130. "An Act to regulate the construction of bridges over navigable waters." March 23, 1906.

When the Gulf, Colorado and Santa Fe Railway definitively selected Gainesville as its northern-most Texas terminus in April of 1886, the 49th U.S. congress authorized construction of a "wagon and foot-bridge over the Red River at Brown's Ferry" the next month.[85] This act granted the right to build a toll bridge to the Gainesville and Chickasaw Bridge Company, which had formed in 1885, with the officers being Gainesville-based businessmen: W. M. Dougherty, J. M. Lindsay, A. E. Dobson, and T. A. Tyler.[86] The bridge, however, was never built, even as an "piggy back" extension to the Santa Fe bridge.[87] This may have been because there simply were no rules or regulations to build such bridges in the late 19th century.

Hope still lingered for an eventual bridge, though. One person who saw the potential was William Killgore, owner of the William Killgore Department Store in Gainesville. In the early 20th century Killgore purchased the land surrounding Sacra's Ferry and by 1918, he had bought the land surrounding Brown's Ferry.

The Toll Bridge
Killgore made a wise decision to purchase Sacra's Ferry. In 1916, several Gainesville businessmen pooled monies to erect a toll bridge across the Red River at the ferry site. The company they formed contracted with the Canadian River Valley Bridge and Construction Company from Oklahoma City to construct a

---

[85] 49th Congress, Session 1, Chapters 354, 355. May 17,1886.
[86] Austin American Statesman, January 27 1885.
[87] This is supposition, bolstered by editorials in contemporary newspapers that lamented the lack of a wagon bridge across the river. I have also not found any extant photographs of the original Santa Fe bridge.

CHAP. 354.—An act granting to the Gainesville and Chickasaw Bridge Company the consent of the United States to construct and maintain a bridge over Red River at or near Brown's Ferry, in Cooke County, Texas.

May 17, 1886.

Be it enacted by the Senate and House of Representatives of the United States of America in Congress assembled, That to the Gainesville and Chickasaw Bridge Company, a corporation created under the laws of Texas by charter filed January twenty-fourth, eighteen hundred and eighty-five, is granted the consent of the Government to construct and maintain for ninety years a bridge, and approaches thereto, over Red River, at or within three miles of Brown's Ferry, in Cooke County, Texas, to be used for the passage of foot-passengers, animals, and vehicles of all kinds, for reasonable rates of toll, to be approved from time to time by the Secretary of War.

Gainesville and Chickasaw Bridge Company authorized to build a wagon and foot-bridge over the Red River at Brown's Ferry, Tex. Tolls.

SEC. 2. That the right herein granted shall be void unless said bridge is constructed within four years from the passage of this act.

To be built within four years.

SEC. 3. That the bridge constructed under this act shall be a lawful structure, and shall be known and recognized as a post-route; and the same is hereby declared to be a post-route upon which also no higher charge shall be made for the transmission over the same of the mails, the troops, and the munitions of war of the United States than other persons pay for like transportation; and the United States shall have the right of way for a postal telegraph across said bridge: *Provided,* That before this act shall take effect said company shall submit to the Secretary of War the plans and specifications of said bridge, showing the proposed location and structure contemplated, and that it shall be decided by the Secretary that said bridge does not and will not ob-

To be a lawful structure and post-route.

Provisos.
Plans, etc., to be approved by Secretary of War.

64   FORTY-NINTH CONGRESS. SESS. I. CHS. 354, 355. 1886.

Right to amend, etc., reserved.
Free navigation not to be obstructed.

struct or impair the navigation of said Red River: *Provided further,* That Congress reserves the right to alter, amend, or repeal this act at any time; and that if at any time navigation of the said river shall in any manner be obstructed or impaired by the said bridge, the Secretary of War shall have authority, and it shall be his duty, to require the said company to alter and change the said bridge, at its own expense, in such manner as may be proper to secure free and complete navigation without impediment; and if upon reasonable notice to said company to make such change or improvements the said company fails to do so, the Secretary of War shall have authority to make the same at the expense of said company, and all rights conferred by this act shall be forfeited; and Congress shall have power to do any and all things necessary to secure the free navigation of the river.

Approved, May 17, 1886.

29. *The 49th U.S. congress authorized a "wagon and foot bridge" to be built over the Red River at Brown's Ferry in 1886, but it never was constructed (Library of Congress).*

"suspension structure several hundred feet long" for $40,000.[88] H. F. Mitchell of the Canadian River Valley Bridge and Construction Company lauded the location at Sacra's Ferry as "an ideal one… the foundations are amply safe to build upon. The banks of the river are of sufficient height that it does not require a lengthy bridge for this place; therefore, the cost of the structure is not exciting."[89] The steep banks that had hindered north/south travel for decades were now considered an asset.

Several meetings were held in Gainesville to encourage investment in the toll bridge. By August of 1917, the Gainesville Red River Bridge Company formed, whose officers included H. W. Stark, J. D. Leeper, F. H. Sherwood, J. C. Whaley, John Mahan, S. M. King, C. C. Littleton, and William McKemie.[90] J. D. Leeper served as the company's vice president. By 1916, he had amassed all of the tracts of land in Love County, Oklahoma around Chriner Lake and Brown's Spring. The president of the company was none other than H. W. Stark, namesake of Stark Ranch. A druggist and owner of a store in downtown Gainesville, Stark had been buying and selling property from and to William Killgore between 1912 and 1916. The transactions amounted to almost two thousand acres.[91] However, Killgore maintained ownership of the Brown and Sacra ferry sites until his death.

---

[88] Daily Ardmoreite, June 13 1916 and Fort Worth Record Telegram, May 13 1916.
[89] Gainesville Daily Register and Messenger, June 7 1916.
[90] Gainesville Daily Register, August 16 1917.
[91] Cooke County Deed records, Deed of Trust 004 p.521. Between December 21, 1912 and January 1, 1916 the following tracts were exchanged between H.W. Stark and William Killgore: J.M. Dickenson Survey (1700 acres), Reed Survey (80 acres), O.K. Ham Survey (20 acres), and G.M Bond Survey (160 acres). All of these transactions, consolidated under one deed of trust, were purchased for one dollar.

Of course, bridges and roads spanning across state boundaries is an interstate commerce transaction, a power exclusively reserved for federal congress. Sam Rayburn, then a young congress person from Texas representing North Texas, sponsored a bill to legitimize the company's enterprise, which became law during the 65th congressional session. In October 1917, the bridge was authorized for the Gainesville Red River Bridge Company "to construct, maintain and operate a bridge… across the Red River at Sacras Ferry… at a point suitable to the interest of navigation."[92]

> **CHAP. 65.**—An Act Granting the consent of Congress to the Gainesville Red River Bridge Company to construct a bridge across Red River.
>
> October 5, 1917. [S. 2816.]
> [Public, No. 52.]
>
> *Be it enacted by the Senate and House of Representatives of the United States of America in Congress assembled,* That the consent of Congress is hereby granted to the Gainesville Red River Bridge Company, or its successors and assigns, to construct, maintain, and operate a bridge and approaches thereto across the Red River at Sacras Ferry, Cooke County, Texas, and Love County, Oklahoma, at a point suitable to the interests of navigation, in accordance with the provisions of the Act entitled "An Act to regulate the construction of bridges over navigable waters," approved March twenty-third, nineteen hundred and six.
>
> SEC. 2. That the right to alter, amend, or repeal this Act is hereby expressly reserved.
>
> Approved, October 5, 1917.

30. *The 65th U.S. Congress authorized the Gainesville Red River company to build a toll bridge at the site of Sacra's Ferry in 1917. (Library of Congress).*

Rapid work on the bridge commenced. The Gainesville Red River Bridge Company awarded the contract to build the bridge to the Midland Bridge Company of Kansas City for $60,000.[93] Upon completion, the five-span iron truss bridge measured 1,455 feet long and stood thirty-five feet above the Red River's low water level. The concrete piers were sunk

---

[92] 65th Congress Session 1, Chapter 65, "An Act Granting the consent of Congress to the Gainesville Red River Bridge Company to construct a bridge across Red River," p 339, 1917. The same congressional session also authorized the erection of a toll bridge across the Red River at Colbert's Ferry above Denison, Grayson County, Texas.
[93] Fort Worth Record Telegram, October 19 1917; Jacksboro News (Jacksboro, TX), October 24 1917.

forty feet down to the bedrock foundation. The approaches on both sides were built on high ground so as to prevent any bridge closures due to high water.[94] The commissioner's court in Cooke County fixed the toll rates at $1.50 per automobile; $1.50 per one ton truck; 75 cents for a four- horse buggy or wagon; 50 cents for a wagon or buggy pulled by two horses; 25 cents per horse and rider; and pedestrians at 10 cents each. Livestock was also charged 25 cents per head.[95]

In March of 1918, Killgore sold a bit over one acre of the Sacra's ferry site to the Gainesville Red River Bridge Company. In July, Killgore purchased the eighty acres parcel that surrounded Brown's Ferry.[96] That same year, J. D. Leeper chartered Leeper Lake to become a private fishing resort.[97] The deep bend of the Red River was poised to become a major thoroughfare. The *Gainesville Daily Register* waxed poetic (and grammatically flawed) about this turn of fortune:

> *"From today Gainesville lays aside the life of yesterday as an experience that has passed. These business men [sic] have injected into her life the power that wins. The past years are but the foundation stones on which the life of the future is builded [sic]. Noble ambition and intelligent effort know no bounds. The Gainesville Gateway Route form the friendly handshake between the Great lakes and the Gulf. Gainesville's greatest achievement in the past has been eclipsed. The riches of yesterday are not to be compared to the fortunes of the morrow. Whatever men dare, they may do."*[98]

---

[94] The Daily Ardmoreite, February 9 1919.
[95] Fort Worth Record Telegram November 1, 1917.
[96] Deed records: No. 2606, William Killgore and wife to Gainesville Bridge Company, No. 6160 A.C. Rose and wife to William Killgore, July 20 1918.
[97] Enid Daily Eagle, June 10 1918.
[98] Gainesville Daily Register, August 16 1917.

In February of 1919, the bridge opened. The state of Oklahoma was busy constructing a highway approach on its end, as the road to the bridge on the northern side of the river was still unimproved. Gainesville had already improved Grand Avenue, the road from the city to Sacra's Ferry, but the state of Texas and Cooke County lacked initiative to extend the improvements southward.

31. The toll bridge opened to great fanfare according to an article, with an accompanying photograph, in the Daily Ardmoreite in February of 1919 (Newspapers.com).

Gainesville, the county seat situated only ten miles from the border but for decades only approachable from the east or west; the city in the middle of the storied Cross Timbers landscape; the city that in the 1860s was on the verge of becoming lost from fear of frontier violence…. was finally connected directly to the north by a bridge that spanned the Red River at the deep bend — the heart of the Stark Ranch.

Chapter 5
Starks at the River

When the Gainesville Red River Bridge Company opened its toll bridge in 1919, the lands surrounding the former ferry sites along the southern shore of the Red River were owned by William Killgore and his second wife, Lucile Spires. Informally known as Lucy, she is the reason why the land along the deep bend is now known as Stark Ranch.

William Killgore marries Lucy Spires
William Killgore was born in Tennessee in 1847 and came to Texas after the Civil War. During the conflict, he served as amounted rifleman in K Company, 22nd Confederate Calvary. Mustered into service on August 4, 1862 in Virginia, Killgore spent most of the war as a prisoner in Indianapolis.[99] Once in Texas, Killgore came to Fannin and Grayson counties before permanently settling in Cooke County with his wife, Mary Dobson, whom he married in 1886.[100] Once in Gainesville, he

---
[99] Ancestry.com; Gainesville Daily Register, April 10 1923.
[100] Ancestry.com

bought several properties throughout the county, many on mortgage. He leased his land to tenants and may have also made some sharecropping arrangements.[101] Killgore built a thriving retail business; eventually, his furniture, department and dry goods stores occupied most of the western three-hundred block of Commerce Street in downtown Gainesville. William and Mary Killgore lived in a stately, turreted bricked Victorian house just up the street from the store, at the northwest corner of Commerce and Scott streets.[102]

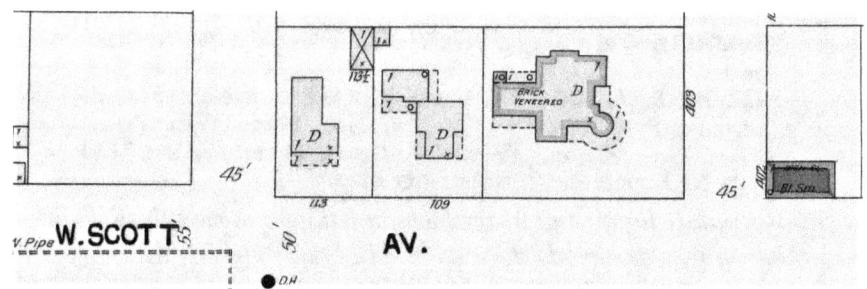

32. The Killgore home at Scott and Commerce Streets, outlined in this 1902 Sanborn Fire Insurance Map, still stands (UT Perry Castaneda Library).

Mary Dobson Killgore died in 1911.[103] Two years later, William Killgore married Lucy Spires, a farmer's daughter who was forty-seven years his junior. The Spires family, consisting of both parents and seven children, had been renting a farm in Arkansas in close proximity of Lucy Spire's maternal grandparents. The family left for Cooke County as part of a caravan in 1905, a journey that Lucy Spires undertook on horseback. Once in Cooke County, they rented land owned by Killgore along the Sacra Ferry Road, where they built a house and a farm that was later used by other

---

[101] Deed Records, Cooke County
[102] City directories, Gainesville Sanborn Maps
[103] Ancestry.com

tenants.[104] The Spires made Cooke County their permanent home; their son Cicero found work as a driver for the Wells Fargo Express, and Lucy married her parents' landlord.[105] According to Lucy, she had met William Killgore when he visited their farm, and he had begun courting her after his wife had passed. Once married, Lucy and William Killgore lived in the house on Commerce Street. The Commerce Street house had been built for William Killgore and Mary Dobson Killgore in 1894.[106]

> mings.
> **KILLGORE WM** (Mary), Pres Wm Killgore Co, r 403 N Commerce.
> **KILLGORE WM CO THE,** Wm Killgore, Pres and Mngr; C P Priddy, First Vice Pres; V H Horton, Second Vice Pres; L J Wynn, Sec and Treas; Dry Goods, Furniture, Etc 313-325 N Commerce. (See left top lines.)

33. *Willian Killgore and Mary Dobson Killgore owned the Killgore Company, a dry goods store, as listed in the 1910 city directory for Gainesville (Cooke County Genealogical Society).*

According to Lucy Spires, William Killgore was best friends with Harlen Stark, another Gainesville businessman. It may have been Stark's influence as the president of the Gainesville Red River Bridge Company that ensured that the toll bridge was erected at the old Sacra's Ferry site on land owned by his friend, William Killgore. Killgore may have also hedged his bets, though; while the toll bridge was still under discussion, he negotiated the purchase of old Brown's Ferry. In 1918, he bought the Brown's Ferry from the Roses, who had acquired the land and the rights to the ferry in 1899.[107]

---

[104] Dallas Morning News, September 5 1978.
[105] City directories
[106] Dallas Morning News, September 5 1978.
[107] Cooke County Deed Records

Probate

William Killgore died in 1923; as he and Lucile Spires had no children of their own, Lucile Spires Killgore was set to inherit everything. There was a hiccup with the probate, though. The will for Killgore's first wife, Mary Dobson Killgore, who died in 1911, had been probated in 1922, with her entire estate bequeathed to William Killgore.[108] When the city's newspaper announced that William Killgore's own will was to be probated in 1923, an objection was raised by Maggie Killgore Horton, William and Mary Killgore's daughter.

34. The Killgore household listed two daughters in the 1880 census. The daughters were first listed as "adopted" but the word was marked out (National Archives).

In 1897, William Killgore and Mary Dobson Killgore formally adopted Maggie and Lucile Holder. The sisters had been born in 1870 and 1874 in Tennessee and had lived with the Killgores since at least 1880, when they were listed in the Grayson County census as "adopted daughters."[109] In either the late 19th or early 20th century, Maggie Holder Killgore married Val Horton, who served as an executive for the William Killgore Department Store. They lived a few blocks from the store and from the Killgore house on Scott Street.

---

[108] Cooke County Probate Records
[109] It is unknown what happened to Lucile Holder.

The couple had a son, William, who later served in World War II.[110]

Maggie Holder Horton appeared in William Killgore's will as "my adopted daughter" but the obituary published in the Gainesville Register did not mention her at all, instead reporting that the deceased "had no children."[111] Maggie Holder Killgore Horton contested the probate of William Killgore's will in 1923. Her suit alleged that she was the "heir and only heir of the said William Killgore, and that she is entitled to inherit the entire estate." She further contended that "William Killgore did not execute" the will and if he did, he would have done so "under the influence and duress of his wife, Lucy Killgore... he did not and could not resist the influence exercised over him." Lastly, Maggie Holder Killgore Horton claimed that William Killgore "did not have sufficient mental capacity to understand and realize" that he was signing his will, and that the "purported will is not acknowledged and witnessed, as required by law."[112]

Lucy Spires Killgore and her attorneys contended that the will was legally written, signed and witnessed in 1920 and that Horton's claim was without merit. However, one of the witnesses to Killgore's will gave a confusing deposition. G. M. Maudlin, a long-time acquaintance of William Killgore and a tenant farmer on Killgore's land near the Red River, stated that while he signed as a witness, he actually didn't see William Killgore sign the will.[113]

---

[110] Census records, city directories
[111] Gainesville Register, April 10 1923.
[112] Cooke County Probate Record, PR 3197 1923.
[113] Ibid. The Probate Record spells the name "Kilgore."

In October 1923, Maggie Holder Killgore Horton withdrew her suit against the will. Instead of receiving $4,000 that the will bequeathed to her, Horton received $7,500 and signed a quit claim deed to Lucy Spires Killgore, which absolved the estate of any debts owed to her. Maggie Holden Killgore Horton died in 1955 and is now buried, like her father and mother, at Fairview Cemetery in Gainesville.

Lucy Spires Killgore marries Harlen Stark
The wealthy widow who now owned the land surrounding Brown's and Sacra's ferries at the deep bend of the Red River did not stay single for long. In November 1923, she married her former husband's friend, Harlen Stark, himself a widower.

Like William Killgore, Harlen Stark attended the Dixon Street Christian Church in Gainesville. Like William Killgore, his second marriage was to a woman many years his junior. And just like William Killgore, Stark was a successful businessman. He owned the H. W. Stark Drug Store in downtown Gainesville. Born in Grayson County in 1867, Stark's father had come from Missouri to Texas before the Civil War and his mother was Texan. Stark married Katie Miller in 1893. They had one daughter, Una Stark, who attended Texas Christian University. Una Stark's first marriage to Ora Ralph Anderson ended in his death during the Great War. She then married William L. Parker, a physician in Wichita Falls and World War I veteran and had two sons. Her children attended Texas Christian University, too.[114]

---

[114] Wichita Falls City Directory, 1934; Una Stark Parker death certificate, February 26 1945; Cooke County History, Past and Present p. 548. Una Stark Parker was educated in Gainesville's finest schools and became a competent piano player, once giving a solo recital in town in 1917. Her first husband, Ora Anderson, was the superintendent of Gainesville schools. He died in France in 1919.

> **STARK HARLIN W** (Kate), Propr H W Stark Drug Co 111-115 N Dixon, r 225 S Dixon.
> **STARK H W DRUG CO**, H W Stark, Propr, Wholesale and Retail Drugs and Druggists' Sundries Dixon cor Commerce and Broadway.

35. Harlen (misspelled Harlin) and Kate Stark owned the Stark Drug Company in downtown as listed in the 1910 city directory for Gainesville (Cooke County Historical Society).

In 1922, Harlen Stark had broken both of his legs while climbing a ladder. As he coalesced, his wife Katie Miller Stark was suddenly incapacitated by a stroke and never regained consciousness. Her obituary lamented that "the death of Mrs. Stark caused a profound sorrow in Gainesville... she was loved of her sincere Christian character manifested in her everyday walks of life." [115]

The following year, Harlen married Lucy Spires Killgore. Their marriage produced four children and lasted until his death in 1944.

The marriage between two of the wealthiest people in Gainesville consolidated business, property, and influence. Lucy Spires Killgore Stark and Harlen W. Stark were married in Hillsboro by their long-time pastor, who had served at the Dixon Street Christian Church in Gainesville before transferring to the congregation in Hillsboro. The coupled returned to Stark's mansion on South Dixon Street after a honeymoon in South Texas and Mexico, where Stark hunted wild turkeys and deer, and resumed their businesses. She took care of the holdings inherited from William Killgore, which included the land at the deep bend of the Red River, and he

---

[115] Gainesville Register, July 20 1922.

36. Harlen and Kate Stark bought a mansion built by cattleman Isaac Cloud along Dixon Street in Gainesville. This became Lucy Spires Killgore Stark's home after she married Harlen in 1923 (Texas Historical Commission).

managed his drug wholesale business. By this time, his enterprise had grown to occupy several buildings in downtown Gainesville, oil well investments, a White Steamer dealership, and the toll bridge company. He also bought land surrounding the land that Lucy Spires Killgore Stark owned. Together, they cobbled together the Stark Ranch, which ultimately encompassed over two thousand acres.

Under Lucy Spires Stark Killgore, Stark Ranch remained a working farm. The last tenants were the Shumachers, who occupied the home that the Spires family had built when they lived as tenants on the land. To Lucy, this land was "the old

37. Harlen and Lucy Stark (Morton Museum).

homeplace." She fished in the river, gardened at the Dixon Street house, and even became one of the state's last, recognized Confederate widows when she applied for her first husband's pension in 1978 after her son was able to verify William Killgore's Civil War military record. Lucy Spires Stark Killgore died in 1979 and is now buried on a hill at Stark Ranch.

The rugged beauty of the Stark Ranch, with open prairie interposed by the gnarly trees of the Cross Timbers, overlooks the Red River along the steep hillsides of the deep bend. It is a peaceful place… except when the trucks and cars roar along Interstate 35, which cuts the western side of the ranch, or the garish lights of the Winstar Casino, one of the world's largest gambling halls, illuminate the night sky just across the river in the Chickasaw Nation. For many years, the deep bend at Stark Ranch hindered north/south travel until two ferries operated simultaneously in the last quarter of the twentieth century, connecting Cooke County to Pickens County. Then, the railroad linked Texas to Indian Territory and the states beyond. In 1919, the toll bridge opened, with traffic flowing between Cooke County and Love County, Texas and Oklahoma. But progress was not done with Stark Ranch; the second industrial revolution made sure of that.

38. *Lucy Spires Killgore Stark applied for, and received, a Confederate widow's pension in 1978. Her first husband, William Killgore, had served during the Civil War (Dallas Morning News).*

Chapter 6
Roads to the River

At the turn to the 20th century, steam locomotion and horse-drawn wagons dominated the way people moved from one place to another. But change was in the air. The "safety bicycle" debuted in the United States in the 1870s. Sporting two equally sized rubber tires and independent pedal and steering mechanisms, this bicycle caused a cycling craze that captivated the country. Men and women from all walks of life took part in this self-propelled freedom (women especially took to this independent form of movement). Bicyclists needed roads to roam, though, and their push for better thoroughfares was echoed by those who owned automobiles. While much fewer in number, automobile owners were by default wealthier and politically connected. Cyclists and motorists sought "good roads," and their movement showed success throughout the Red River Valley, especially during World War I.

Toll Bridges

The Great War (1914 to 1919; in the U.S., 1917 to 1919) had demonstrated that a need existed for better transportation routes. The railroads which were used to transport equipment, supplies, and troops during the war threatened to be precarious options due to labor strikes and unrest. President Woodrow Wilson had nationalized the railroads to mitigate the logistical problems, but this action did not sit well with capitalists. The advent of the Good Roads Movement led by bicyclists and motorists provided the perfect solution to build profit-making infrastructure while also undermining the railroads' and unions' monopolies on long-distance transports. Coupled with the allure of extending the "Lakes to the Gulf Highway," the name given to the Gainesville to Ardmore road that was now being upgraded into an automobile trail, the prospect of a route independent from railroads, their rates, and their labor troubles made economic sense.[116]

39. The toll bridge at Sacra's Ferry site in 1919 (Morton Museum).

---

[116] Gainesville Daily Register and Messenger, November 8 1916.

Stark Ranch of Cooke County, Texas: History that spans the Red River

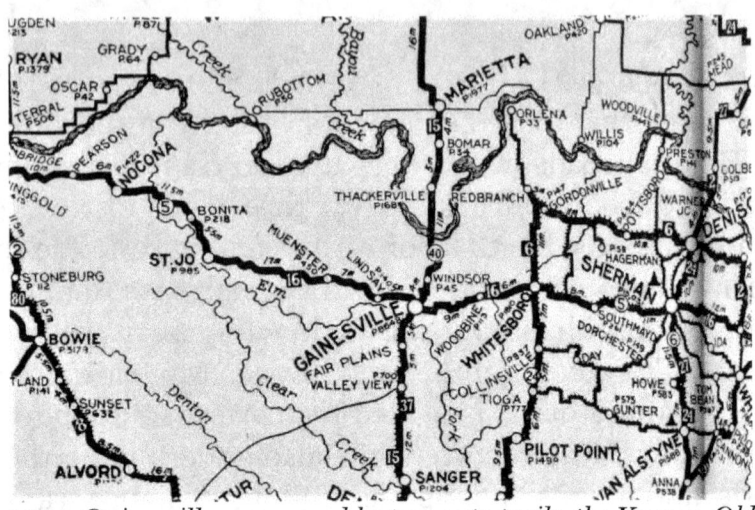

40. *By 1924, Gainesville was served by two auto trails: the Kansas-Oklahoma-Texas Highway (today, U. S. 77) and the North Texas Highway (today, U.S. 82). In Texas, the Kansas-Oklahoma-Texas Highway was also known as the Hobby Highway. Note the dotted lines on this Rand McNally map; the southern portion of this road was not paved (David Rumsey).*

Toll bridges offered this investment option. During and after the Great War, toll bridges were built and opened all across the Red River Valley between Texas and Oklahoma. They were mostly composed of iron or wooded trusses and wooden planks that investors selected from catalog options. Modern toll bridges were erected at Telephone, Fannin County, Texas; at Sowell's Bluff north of Bonham, Texas; between Denison and Durant at Colbert, Oklahoma; between Woodville, Oklahoma and Preston, Texas at the confluence of the Washita River; at Illinois Bend, Texas and at Red River Station, Texas near the old Abilene Cattle Trail Crossing; between Ringgold, Texas and Terral, Oklahoma; north of Petrolia and Byers, Texas; three connecting the oil fields surrounding Grandfield, Oklahoma to the oil fields around Burkburnett, Texas; between Vernon, Texas and Altus, Oklahoma near the old Western Cattle Trail Crossing; between Quanah, Texas and

Eldorado, Oklahoma; and the "moonshiner" between Goodlett, Texas and Hollis, Oklahoma at the 100th meridian.[117]

Toll bridges and the improved roads that brought travelers to them siphoned traffic away from the ferries, where access remained along unimproved roads in the nooks and crannies of the Red River. Gradually, the ferries began disappearing, but some in Cooke County remained operational until the 1930s. They were beloved features of river life.

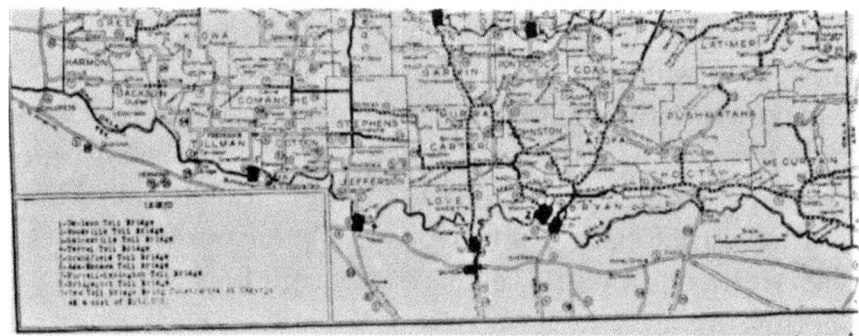

41. In 1929, Harlow's Weekly out of Oklahoma City listed most of the toll bridges across the Red River (Newspapers.com).

Cooke County Ferries

At the turn of the 20th century, the Red River between Cooke and Love counties was serviced by several ferries. Most, like Brown's Ferry and Sacra's Ferry, had been around for several decades and were named for their ferry operators. Starting

---

[117] This list is not exhaustive. The toll bridge between Durant, Oklahoma and Denison, Texas at Colbert replaced the earlier wooden too bridge that initially had been built in 1875 and had to be replaced several times due to flash flooding. Other toll bridges across the Red River between Oklahoma and Texas were proposed but not all were built; for example, in 1913 a bridge at Charlie in Clay County, Texas was proposed but did not come to fruition. The "moonshiner" bridge along the Prairie Dog Town Fork of the Red River in northwest Texas was so named because, according to lore, it was mainly used by local distillers.

from the eastern county line, travelers could use either the Delaware Bend Ferry, Tuck's Ferry (later, Thompson's Ferry), Sacra's Ferry, Brown's Ferry, Freeman's Ferry, the Burneyville Ferry, Warren's Bend Ferry, Hobbs Ferry, Rock Bluff Ferry, or the Courtney Ferry. A few fords were also still used to cross the river until the automobile age made them archaic.[118]

Like Brown's and Sacra's Ferry, interesting stories surrounded the Cooke County ferries and their operators. John Tuck, the ferry operator, and his son Cuburt, for example, became murder victims in 1925. The story was sensationalized in newspapers of the time because it involved an apparent love triangle between Cuburt, a woman of "unknown background," and a man who was also interested in her. John Tuck, who had retired from the operation to work in Cuburt's restaurant, got caught in the middle of a revenge shooting between the competing lovers.

The Burneyville Ferry was one of the most historic ferries in the area as it served the Burney Institute, a boarding school for Chickasaw girls that was established by the Presbytery and the Chickasaw Nation in 1859 (the original rock building still stands on private property). The ferry at Warren's Bend was named after Abel Warren, a fur trader from Massachusetts, who established his second trading post along the Red River at the site near Cache Creek in 1842. His first store, a wooden stockade, was on the southern shore of the river in Fannin County and served as the county seat until Grayson County was carved from Fannin in 1846. The ferry at Delaware Bend got its name from a settlement of Delawares who were

---

[118] The list is not exhaustive. Much of the list is gleaned from a 1901 USGS Soil Survey Map.

removed from the land once Anglos began to claim it. According to Hal Dick who lived near the ferry while it was still operational, outlaws like William Quantrill, Jesse James, and Bonnie and Clyde crossed the river at Delaware Bend.[119]

42. *An unidentified ferry crossing at the Red River (Stark Ranch Collection).*

Ferries in Cooke County ceased operating by the 1930s when free bridges provided motorists unobstructed paths.[120] The bridges became conduits for the federalized highway system that had gained traction in the 1920s.

Free Bridges

By the late 1920s, one free bridge, under federal oversight, had already replaced a toll bridge across the Red River at Arthur City (Lamar County, Texas).[121] Three other free bridges were

---
[119] Gainesville Register, December 22 2014.
[120] Pedestrians were ignored in the planning of highways.
[121] Ardmore Daily Press, November 4 1924. The first free bridge between Texas and Oklahoma was at Arthur City, which connected Hugo, Oklahoma to Paris, Texas. The toll bridge that had been built earlier was poorly constructed and washed away in a flood.

slated to be built in 1925 and 1926 at Davidson (Tillman County, Oklahoma) and Burkburnett (Wichita County, Texas) but injunctions, brought by a lawsuit from the toll bridge operator, stopped the proposals.[122] Injunctions like these played out into the early 1930s, when the Gainesville and Red River Bridge Company's own toll bridge contended with the public's desire for free bridges.

In addition to wanting access the federal highways, the desire for free bridges between Texas and Oklahoma stemmed from disputes over toll fees. Attorney generals from both states argued in April of 1928 that the tolls charged were "arbitrary, unjust and excessive."[123] By 1929, the Secretary of War[124] ordered the tolls charged by the Gainesville Red River Bridge Company, which operated the toll bridge at Stark Ranch, to be reduced. The order resulted from an audit that compared receipts from the Gainesville Red River Bridge Company to the Preston-Woodville Bridge; Cooke County tolls were twenty times higher.[125] That same year, Congress voted to replace the toll bridges with free bridges with Senate Bill No. 75, which authorized removal under eminent domain.

The toll bridge companies, including the Gainesville Red River Bridge Company, protested the forced rate reductions

---

[122] Big Pasture News (Grandfield, OK), September 18 1925 and The Vernon Record (Vernon, TX), April 7 1925.
[123] Victoria Advocate (Victoria, TX), April 4 1928.
[124] The Mayfield-Newton Act of 1927 placed interstate road and bridge construction under the duties of the Secretary of War.
[125] Fort Worth Record Telegram, January 4 1929. The order was also extended to the Red River Bridge Company, which operated the toll bridge between Durant, Oklahoma and Denison, Texas, due to a similar discrepancy.

and sought injunctions to restore the fees in 1930.[126] They argued that the impending construction of free bridges had placed a moratorium on their bridge's earning capacities. A very unique "bridge war" ensued.

43. *The toll bridge booth and house at Sacra's Ferry listed the toll rates. At this point, the bridge had been closed in order to divert traffic to the free bridge a mile upstream (Morton Museum).*

Red River Bridge War

The toll bridge that spanned the Red River between Durant, Oklahoma and Denison, Texas had an older history than any other toll bridge along the Red River. Benjamin Colbert, a Chickasaw national who operated a hotel, plantation, and ferry at the river, erected the original toll bridge in 1875; he rebuilt it at least twice due to flash floods washing the structure away. The bridge was later owned by his heirs. In 1891, Frank Colbert and other men from Texas incorporated as the Red River Bridge Company to build a modern toll bridge that connected the both the Jefferson and the King of Trails

---

[126] Austin American Statesman, August 2 1930 and Fort Worth Star Telegram, November 14, 1930.

Highways.[127] When the Secretary of War required the reduction of toll bridge fees starting in 1929, the Red River Bridge Company did not comply. Instead, the company sought an injunction against the reduction of tolls and the construction of a free bridge – it argued that the federal government did not have jurisdiction.

Building the free bridge commenced, anyway. In 1930, Congress listened to the testimonies of toll bridge owners. The federal government argued that the bridges had been built completely on Indian land and were therefore not subject to state highway mandates or toll contracts, but the bridge company must abide by toll rates set by the War Department.[128] The Red River Bridge Company argued that it possessed a contract with the Texas Highway Commission, which had agreed to buy the bridge and pay out its unexpired contract.

When the free bridge opened in July 1931, the Red River Bridge Company filed an injunction to recuperate the monies contracted for its use by the state of Texas. This led the governor of Texas, Ross Sterling, to erect temporary barricades at the free bridge to prevent interstate traffic from using it until the case was resolved. The governor of Oklahoma, William "Alfalfa Bill" Murray, ordered the Oklahoma Highway Department to remove the barricades by claiming, rightfully, that the bridge was solely under Oklahoma's jurisdiction because it spanned the Red River, which belonged to the state as per the Louisiana Purchase

---

[127] Gainesville Daily Hesperian, October 30 1891.
[128] Committee on Interstate and Foreign Commerce, 71st Congress, 2nd Session, 1930.

Stark Ranch of Cooke County, Texas: History that spans the Red River

44. Oklahoma Governor "Alfalfa" Bill Murray inspects the troops at the Red River Bridge Company's toll bridge between Colbert and Denison during the "war" in 1931 (Oklahoma Historical Society).

Treaty. Sterling sent the Texas Rangers to restore the barricades, which prompted Murray to order the destruction of the road to the toll bridge on the Oklahoma side.

Citizens on both sides of the river opposed the actions of the Red River Bridge Company and the Texas governor. After the Texas legislature lifted the injunction (which meant that the Red River Bridge Company could sue the Texas Highway Commission), a federal judge issued a new order. He demanded that Murray restore access to the toll bridge on the Oklahoma side as the destruction of the road impeded interstate commerce. Instead, Murray declared martial law along the Red river between the free and toll bridges and sent the Oklahoma National Guard to patrol the bridges, even on the Texas side. This "war" was finally resolved when the free bridge opened in late July and the bridge company's suit against Texas was settled.

Since some of the owners of the Red River Bridge Company were also some of the owners of the Gainesville Red River Bridge Company (including H. W. Stark), the controversy at the U. S. 75 bridge could have been easily replicated at Stark Ranch. However, the polemic surrounding the free bridge between Love and Cooke Counties took a different approach.

Route 77/ S. H. 40 Bridge Opens
By 1930, construction of the free bridge across the Red River at Stark Ranch was in full swing. At this point, the road that connected to the free bridge was designated State Highway 40 (Gainesville to Ardmore Highway) by both Texas and Oklahoma. Before 1925, it was known as the "Lakes to Gulf Highway" and on maps, the Hobby Highway.[129] In 1925, the road had received federal money to become Route No. 77, an interstate thoroughfare that connected Sioux City, Iowa to Dallas, Texas,[130] but construction funds were slow to disperse. This is why, while the new free bridge, called the Gainesville-Marietta bridge, was being built to connect the north to the south at Stark Ranch, there was (yet again) no decent road south of Gainesville.

When the free bridge between Cooke and Love Counties at Stark Ranch opened in 1931, the toll bridge still hummed with business. This was because its southern road actually led somewhere. The new Gainesville-Marietta bridge was inaccessible not due to toll disputes but because of poor road

---

[129] Auto Trails Map, Rand McNally and Company, 1924 p. 408-409.
[130] Oklahoma Department of Transportation, Memorial Highways: U.S. 77

45. *The free bridge across the Red River in 1942 (Morton Museum)*

construction. The *Daily Oklahoman* reported that, while the road from Oklahoma City to the Red River was complete and usable, "the main difficulty lies in the fact that the earthen fill on the Texas side of the stream has settled approximately five feet below the bridge roadway… it will have to be brought up to floor level before it can be used. Even if this was passable, the present road from the approach to the existing highway is little more than a trail."[131]

Funding for the construction of a good roadbed for S. H. 40 (U. S. 77) in Texas was delayed due to an injunction filed by "a group of Gainesville citizens" which included shareholders in the Gainesville Red River Bridge Company. Their argument appeared to be that the new road bypassed Gainesville "by two miles." Anger against the delay developed in Fort Worth and other points south of Gainesville, where a free bridge with

---

[131] Daily Oklahoman, July 17 1931.

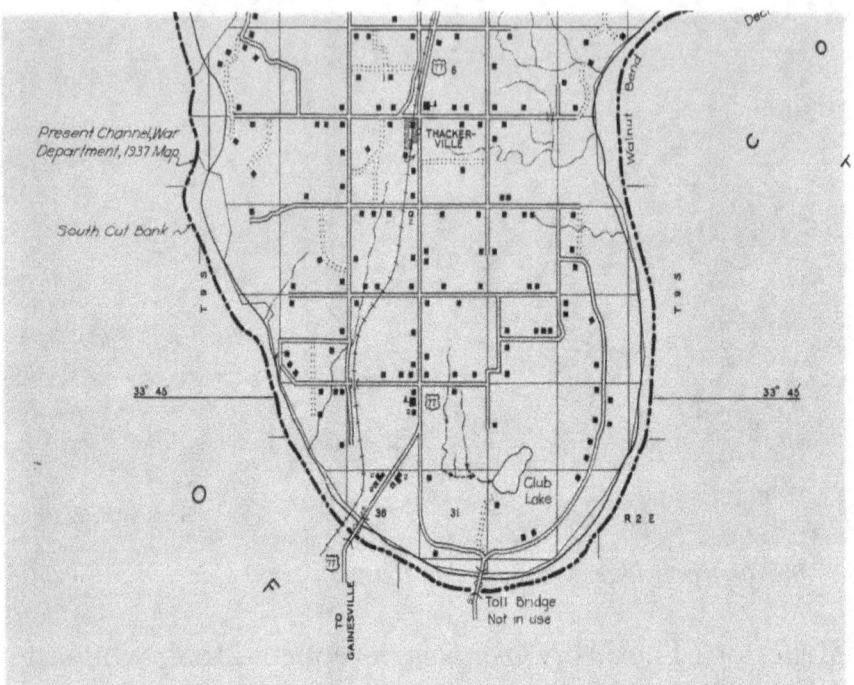

46. *The relative locations of the toll bridge and the free bridge are identified in this 1936 map (Oklahoma State University).*

good approaches in both directions was paramount to economic development.[132] Governor Murray of Oklahoma even offered his state's road equipment to Texas to aid construction.[133] Oklahoma had already lent its surveyors to Texas to help build the road,[134] but the latest offer apparently embarrassed Texas lawmakers. Senator J. J. Loy (Sherman) and Representative C. F. Sullivan (Gainesville) authored a funding bill,[135] and unlike the Red River Bridge Company that owned the toll bridge between Durant, Oklahoma and Denison, Texas, the owners of the toll bridge at Stark Ranch

---

[132] Fort Worth Star Telegram, July 19 1931.
[133] Fort Worth Star Telegram, July 23 1931.
[134] Fort Worth Star Telegram, July 25 1931.
[135] Fort Worth Star Telegram, July 24 1931.

did not oppose this; they had even "offered to pay part of the cost of building a temporary road needed on the Texas side."[136]

This generous offer was most likely made because a buy-out for the toll-bridge's contract would net the Gainesville Red River Bridge Company $150,000 from the Texas Highway Commission. The contract between the company and the state of Texas resolved that if the Secretary of War refused to allow the toll bridge to increase its rates, the Texas Highway Commission would extend the bridge's operating time, and delay the opening of the free bridge, in order to recuperate the losses until the contract's time limit had been reached. Then, the toll bridge would be turned over to the state and the free bridge could be opened. The same contract had been issued to the Terral Bridge Company which operated the toll bridge between Jefferson and Montague Counties. Loy and Sullivan's bill helped to mitigate these "poor contracts;" Loy's office audited the Gainesville Red River Bridge Company's receipts and realized that the contracts' promise of paying the company $10,000 per month to offset loss toll revenue was overblown… he did not admit the amount was fraudulent but alluded to it.[137]

Gainesville citizens, nervous that this huge sum might delay the opening, "raised funds by contribution to build the three-mile detour from Highway No. 77 to the short, completed section of Highway No. 40, which will enable use of the bridge" and also placed the approach to the free bridge through the western part of Gainesville, thus placating all

---

[136] Blackwell Journal Tribune (Blackwell, OK), July 25 1931; Fort Worth Star Telegram, July 25 1931
[137] Fort Worth Star Telegram, June 14 1931.

Stark Ranch of Cooke County, Texas: History that spans the Red River

47. *By the late 1950s, a second bridge was built next to the iron truss "free bridge" as traffic had increased, and U. S. 77 was slated to become a "super highway" (Stark Ranch Collection).*

sides of the argument.[138] This action did the trick. The free bridge between Cooke and Love Counties along U. S. 77, S. H. 40 finally opened on the first week of September 1931. The bridge's opening sparked a massive celebration on both sides of the river, with the *Fort Worth Star Telegram* exalting:

> *"Opening the structure marks another important step in the elimination of toll bridges which in the past have laid a tax upon highway travel. It is not, of course, that these toll bridges did not render a service well justifying the tax; indeed, they were built, in nearly every instance, as a public convenience by public-spirited citizens who deserved and receive the gratitude of the public... But the day of the toll bridge has passed, just as the day of the toll road passed long before."* [139]

---

[138] Fort Worth Star Telegram, July 26 1931.
[139] Fort Worth Star Telegram, September 7 1931.

The toll bridge was now defunct. The last of the lawsuits filed against the states by the Red River Bridge Company were settled by 1936; the bridge companies, including the Gainesville Red River Bridge Company, were awarded the remainder of their Texas contracts.[140] The toll bridges between Denison, Texas and Durant, Oklahoma; Gainesville, Texas and Marietta, Oklahoma; and Ringgold, Texas and Terral, Oklahoma, were dynamited and destroyed.

---

[140] Austin American Statesman, January 31 1936.

Chapter 7
The River as a Resource

When the free bridge across the Red River opened in north of Gainesville in 1931 (and was later replaced with modern structures in the 1950s and 1980s), the river was no longer much of a barrier. Before the free bridge, travelers had to contend with nature; whether they crossed on ferries or forded in shallower waters, they had to mind the swift currents. When they crossed over toll bridges, they had to pay the fees and mind the other traffic before they could traverse the bridge safely. Today, interstate travel has made these concerns almost obsolete. Cars and trucks zoom on the modern U. S. 77, now known as Interstate 35, and breach the river easily and without much thought. The 20th century made the river, which never was a transportation conduit in Cooke County, into a resource instead. In Louisiana, Texas and Oklahoma, "Red River Valley" authorities were established to develop the economic and geographic potential of the river.

Lake Texoma

The Red River has flooded catastrophically several times in the valley between Oklahoma and Texas. The 1888 flood wiped out several Gulf, Colorado & Santa Fe Railway bridges, although not its Red River bridge. The 1908 flood affected all of the rivers in north Texas and southern Oklahoma — it's the reason why most railroad bridges were replaced by 1911.[141] The historic 1927 flood that affected the Mississippi River also left its mark in the Red River Valley. Calls for damming the river "for flood control and navigation"[142] began in earnest in early 20th century in Louisiana. The talk of creating a reservoir, however, shifted to Texas.

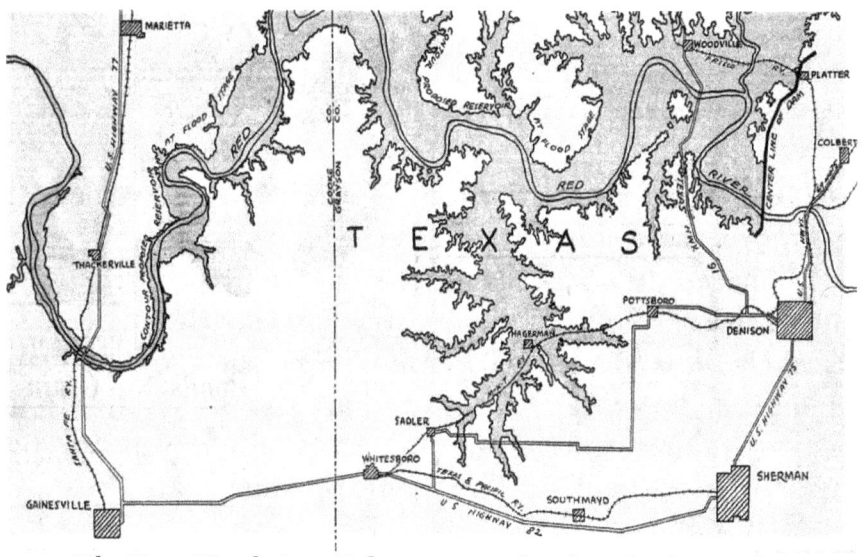

48. *The Fort Worth Star Telegram speculated on the dammed river's reach in this 1938 speculative map (Newspapers.com).*

---

[141] The disastrous 1908 flood birthed Dallas's "Kessler Plan," an urban design that Dallas follows to this day. The plan straightened the Elm Fork of the Trinity River through downtown Dallas with a continuous levee. The reclaimed riverbed was built into Interstate 35.

[142] The Times (Shreveport, LA), June 16 1908 and July 21 1927.

Stark Ranch of Cooke County, Texas: History that spans the Red River

Sam Rayburn, the Speaker of the U.S. House of Representatives, was a Democrat from Bonham, Fannin County, Texas. His legislation helped secure the toll bridges over the Red River in various places after World War I, and he continued to champion projects that economically benefitted his home region throughout his career. President Franklin Delano Roosevelt could not have moved forward on much of the New Deal legislation without Sam Rayburn's support and deal making. Rayburn, who never once took money from lobbyists, was keen on duplicating the success of the Tennessee River Valley Authority program in Texas. The Red River was a perfect place to do this. After the U.S. Army Corps of Engineers settled the location of the dam at the confluence of the Red and Washita rivers at Baer's Ferry north of Denison, over $54 million was eventually allocated to build a bi-state reservoir aptly named Lake Texoma.

Completed in 1944, Lake Texoma stretches over five counties, including Cooke County, and covers about three hundred and twelve square miles. Its fed not only by the Red River, but also by the Washita River as well as Rock Creek, Glass Creek, Big Mineral Creek, and Little Mineral Creek. The Denison Dam is one hundred sixty five feet high and almost three miles long. Over two hundred thirty thousand acres of land was purchased to make way for the lake. The towns of Hagerman, Preston Bend, Woodville and Aylesworth were removed as were numerous cemeteries and sixty-four miles of railroad tracks.[143]

The creation of Lake Texoma did not impact the Stark Ranch directly. Only at flood stage would the Red River at the deep bend become wider, but not by much. The lake, however,

---

[143] Fort Worth Star Telegram, August 26 1938.

promised a steady water supply and recreational opportunities. Lucy Stark recognized the potential for a civic project. She offered to donate land at the head of Pecan Creek at the Stark Ranch to the City of Gainesville in the hopes of building a reservoir.[144] The city chose to dam Fish Creek instead and developed Hubert H. Moss Lake in the 1960s.

Stark Ranch's role in developing a regional water supply was not over, though. Lucy Stark was not the only person who had recognized the need for a reservoir to supply Cooke County's water during the historic drought along the Red River Valley in the 1950s.

The Red River Pump Station
The Red River Valley experienced one of the worst dry periods in the early 1950s, when rainfall stayed away during the first half of the decade. This drought was much worse than the one that fed the Dust Bowl of the 1930s and fear of catastrophic water shortages led to a record number of reservoirs built throughout North Texas, all of which were championed by Sam Rayburn during the Eisenhower Administration. The drought ushered the development of Lewisville Lake, Lake Lavon, Lake Ray Hubbard, and Grapevine Lake in the North Texas region.

Before these lakes were built, though, anxiety about the future of its water supply had left the City of Dallas in a fever pitch. At this time, the citizens of this growing metropolis were fed by Bachman Lake, White Rock Lake, and Lake Dallas in Denton County.[145] In 1952, only a four-month water supply remained at Lake Dallas; Dallas faced severe rationing. The

---

[144] Communication with Lucy Stark Sutton by Stark Ranch, July 13 2016.
[145] K.H. Hoefle to W.S. McDonald. City of Dallas Memorandum, March 26 1954.

city devised a plan to pump water from the Red River through Pecan Creek. Since Pecan Creek emptied into the Elm Fork of the Trinity River which was dammed at Lake Dallas, engineers hoped to increase the city's water supply with Red River water.[146] The pump station would naturally be placed at Stark Ranch, where Pecan Creek originated.

49. *The pump station was built along the river by the city of Dallas in 1954 (Dallas Municipal Archives).*

---

[146] Sweetwater Reporter (Sweetwater, TX), October 19 1952.

IN TEST OPERATION
Red River Joins Lake Dallas

Muddy, reddish waters of Red River were expected to flow into the upper end of Lake Dallas today.

The engineering feat, that some skeptics said would never be completed, pumps water out of Red River, about 40 miles north of Lake Dallas, into Pecan Creek, about six miles north of Gainesville. Gravity then takes care of the stream flow, carrying it southward though the heart of Gainesville and thence into Elm Creek, just south of that city.

Elm Creek (Elm Fork of the Trinity River) brings it through the south part of Cooke County, into Denton County and, flowing under the Highway 24 bridge east of Denton, finally emptying into Lake Dallas.

The operation is being staged in order to bolster Dallas' dwindling water supply. Lake Dallas is the city's chief source of water for drinking and industrial uses.

The waters of Red River are pumped "uphill" into Pecan Creek by giant pumps at Dallas' million-dollar pumping station. Four giant pumps are reported doing the work. The station is located six miles north of Gainesville on the Stark Ranch and the water is pumped approximately two miles through a 48 inch pipe to the headwaters of Pecan Creek.

Karle Hoefle, Dallas waterworks superintendent, explained that the current operation is merely a test, to determine the reliability of the pumps and also to determine how much of the Red River water actually will reach Lake Dallas.

After the current 30-day tests are completed, the Dallas City Council is expected to decide how much Red River water should be pumped to Lake Dallas. Officials of Dallas said it probably would take two or three days for the waters to complete the 4-mile "run."

See RED RIVER, Page 2

50. For decades, politicians and civic leaders had hoped to join the Red River with Texas river systems in the hopes of navigation. While not about navigation, using the river as a resource led to a partial realization of the dream (February 1954, Denton Record Chronicle).

In September of 1953, the City of Dallas approved the installation of a pumping station at the Red River and awarded the construction contract to the Kellner Jetty Company out of Kansas City. The pumping station consisted of six intakes powered by six turbines at the old Brown's Ferry site at Stark Ranch. A large pipeline was buried into the hill above the old ferry site, where the pumped water flowed into Pecan Creek's spring. The entire pumping system, which ferried approximately seventy-nine million gallons a day, acted like a small hydroelectric dam, generating its own electricity. The Starks received nominal compensation from the City of Dallas to gain access to the shore of Red River and Pecan Creek as the station commenced operation in March of 1954. However, three problems quickly emerged.

51. *Pecan Creek flooded often due to the water pumped from the Red River into the Elm Fork of the Trinity River (Dallas Municipal Archives).*

As the station pumped Red River water into Pecan Creek, the creek naturally swelled. This posed a problem along a low water crossing at Gordon Street in Gainesville, which became continuously inundated. In April of 1954, Gainesville authorized the construction of a culvert at Gordon Street, which Dallas paid $5,000 for.[147] However, continued setbacks exacerbated the problem. A suit was filed about the dangerous crossing; cattle were swimming to neighboring pastures along the bridge; and a schoolboy nearly drowned at Gordon Street when he was swept away by the swift current. An anonymous note originating from the water department of the City of Dallas lamented, "We are going to get in trouble if this is not remedied."

Flooding constituted an additional problem. Pecan Creek, already subject to flash flooding, became even more unstable due to increased water levels as Red River water was pumped into the stream. Engineer K.H. Hoefle recommended that to

---

[147] City of Dallas Municipal Archives

avoid catastrophic flooding, pumping be "suspended during the months of April and May, and possibly June." These three months, however, were also the most productive in terms of water supply and water quality. The solution was to only use one or two pumps at any given time.

The third problem proved the most insurmountable one: the amount of salt contained in the Red River left its water undrinkable. Henry Graeser, superintendent of Dallas's water department, informed Robert S. Kerr, U.S. senator from Oklahoma, about the salinity, explaining that the "chloride content of our city water rose as high as 1,220 ppm in some areas... the U.S. Public Health Service recommends the maximum of 250 ppm." Kerr was intensely interested in developing rivers as drinking water supplies and as navigation conduits. He welcomed Graeser's suggestion of "reducing the natural and man-made pollution in the Red River."[148] Kerr asked Graeser to testify before the House of Representatives Appropriations Committee to explain the need for desalination and pollution controls. Pollution controls included containing brines from oil field developments.

Red River Authority
Congress thus authorized the Red River Authority of Texas in 1960 "in order to protect, preserve and, when necessary, restore the purity and sanitary condition of the surface waters of Red River and its tributaries."[149] Unfortunately, the authority was not funded; it relied on contributions by

---

[148] Henry Graeser to Robert Kerr, April 6 1959. Robert Kerr proposed building canals that would link the Red River to the Trinity River in the hopes of building industrial infrastructure. His vision was not extended into Texas but was realized with the development of ports on the Verdigris River in Oklahoma.
[149] Red River Authority Rules and Regulations, July 1960.

52. Red River Authority was formed in 1960 to control and protect the Red River (Stark Ranch Collection).

interested parties, including from its board of directors.[150] The authority's first act was to order a pollution survey of the river, which discovered high volumes of salt discharged from oil field disposal wells. The survey also reported on "natural pollution" of the river stemming from salt deposits in the canyons at the river's source.[151]

Although the City of Dallas maintained interest in supplementing its water supply with the Red River, the authority's pollution report derived the conclusion that

---

[150] John Anderson to Henry Graeser, March 10 1961.
[151] C.C. Glenn to Members of the Board of Directors, Red River Valley Authority, 1960.

expenses associated with desalination would be prohibitive. The city eventually sought other options for its water supply, including buying water rights to Garza-Little Elm Lake (now, Lewisville Lake, which was created out of an expansion of Lake Dallas); Grapevine Lake; Ray Roberts Lake; Lake Tawakoni; and Lake Fork. Another nail-in-the-coffin to the City of Dallas's Red River pumping station was a lawsuit filed by Lucy Stark against the city's easement for the pipeline.

The Red River Pumping Station at Stark Ranch had a promising beginning but was plagued by problems from the very start. By 1962, the city had stopped using the station and eventually, the machinery was dismantled. Only the concrete structure that supported the turbines remains, which the current owners of Stark Ranch have made into a picnic area. The attempt at making the Red River a potable stream had failed.

Chapter 8
Schmitzes at the Red River

Today, Stark Ranch is owned and managed by John Schmitz and his family. The Schmitzes bought the ranch from the heirs to Lucy Stark as corporate transactions. A shrewd businesswoman, Lucy Spires Killgore Stark had incorporated the ranch and gifted shares to her children. They, in turn, sold their shares to the Schmitzes. In a nod to history and preservation, the Schmitz family retained Stark Ranch as the name of this beautiful piece of land.

German Roots
The Schmitzes are German people who made their home in Cooke County at the turn of the 20th century. But they weren't the only Germans to claim the area around Gainesville. Cooke County has one of Texas's most prolific German immigrant communities. Their *herkunft* (ancestry) is unique to the state; unlike the better-known Hill Country Germans,[152] the Cross

---
[152] The "Hill Country Germans" are ethnically German people who entered Texas directly, either at Galveston or Indianola, in an immigration scheme sponsored by the

Timber Germans who settled North Texas are mostly Westphalians who first immigrated to German settlements in Illinois, Iowa, Missouri, Minnesota, and Wisconsin. They entered Texas after the Civil War because land was cheap, and because settlement was encouraged by the Catholic Church and the Flusche Brothers. Emil and August Flusche founded a colonization company in Texas in the prairie west of Gainesville that would entice railroads to connect western Texas in a period that coincided with the aftermath of the Red River Wars between the U.S. military and Southern Plains tribes.[153] Their colony centered on the town of Muenster, which was named for the capital of the German principality, Westphalia, and is now the capital of the German *Bundesstaat* (federal state), North-Rhine Westphalia.

The first Schmitz arrived in Illinois from Pinn, Westphalia, Germany. William Joseph Schmitz's immigration coincided with the consolidation and unification of Germany under Otto von Bismarck, which led to several wars, protestant-dominated state theology in traditionally Catholic regions, and the privatization of communal lands. Thousands of Germans left their homes and immigrated to the United States due to the economic and religious stresses this social upheaval caused.

Adelsverein. The *Adelsverein* consisted of a group of aristocrats who piggy-backed on the tales of successful Germans who settled in Stephen F. Austin's Mexican colony in the early 1830s. In the 1840s, the *Adelsverein* paid for land in the hill country between Austin and San Antonio, then colonized it with mostly destitute people from their principalities and dukedoms. Many of the commoners were fleeing from the German revolutions of the mid-19th century, which created wide-spread famines and emptied entire villages by forced conscription.

[153] The Red River Wars (1871-1875; most intense, 1874-1875) resulted in the removal of Comanches, Apaches, Kiowas, Cheyennes, Arapahos, and Wichitas from their homelands in the Cross Timbers and Staked Plains. The U.S. government forced the remnants of the tribes to settle in the Fort Sill reservation. A law passed in 1876 forbade any members of the tribes from entering Texas.

Stark Ranch of Cooke County, Texas: History that spans the Red River

They settled among other Germans in colonies sponsored and encouraged by previous Germans.

William Joseph Schmitz and his wife, Catherine Neu Schmitz, moved with their large family from Iowa to Lindsay, Cooke County, Texas in 1898 to join their kin, the Walterscheids, who had moved to Muenster earlier. Here, the Schmitzes set up prosperous farms and helped to build the religious community of Lindsay. Their second son was John William Schmitz, who married Mary Bezner, a German-American woman from Iowa, in at the Saint Peter's Catholic Church in 1911. In this period, the Schmitzes continued to practice German customs of lively and sumptuous wedding festivities, most likely with accordion music, dancing, and *gemütlichkeit*. This couple had eight children, one of whom was John Henry Schmitz.

53. *The Schmitz family, relocated from Iowa to Cooke County, continued celebrating their ethnic roots, as this Gainesville Register article explains (Cooke County Library).*

Big John's Joints

Born in 1924, John Henry Schmitz, at times nicknamed "Big John" or "Johnny," joined the Merchant Marines in 1943 and later, worked in various capacities in the oil fields. After serving during the Korean Conflict with the "Wolfhounds" (he enlisted in the 27th Infantry Regiment and served as part of the 25th Infantry Division), he returned to Cooke County in 1954 and married Albina Mages at the Sacred Heart church in Muenster.

Albina's parents moved from Westphalia, Iowa to Muenster before she was born. Her paternal grandparents immigrated to the United States in 1891; her grandfather was from Bohemia and her grandmother from Prussia. Albina's mother was German, too. Her mother, Theresa Bayer Mages, was the eldest of a very large family who left mid-western German settlements to farm in Cooke County. Albina was most likely named for her maternal grandmother, Abalonia Fischer (Apolonia Fisher) Bayer, whose family immigrated to Wisconsin from Prussia in the 1870s. Abalonia Fischer Bayer lived with Theresa Bayer Mages and her family when the Mages family moved to Texas.

John Schmitz and Albina Mages Schmitz opened businesses on U. S. 77 across the Red River in Love County, Oklahoma: "Johnny's DX Truck Stop" and "Johnny's B-29" bar.[154] Johnny Schmitz most likely chose the location of these establishments due to the traffic on U. S. 77 because it, in part, mirrored the old "Whiskey Trail," which Texas bootleggers used to bring liquor into the Indian Territory. This time, however, the spirits flowed southward. Despite the lifting of federal

---

[154] Communication with Joseph Schmitz, December 27 2020.

prohibition in 1933, Cooke County voted itself dry in 1936 as Texas counties maintained sovereignty over the sale of alcohol (defined as spirits, wine, and beer) within their boundaries. This changed in 1959, when the Texas Supreme Court transferred that sovereignty to cities and precincts within the counties. Muenster became the first Cooke County town to vote in favor of wine and beer sales immediately after the decision, but selling mixed drinks, cocktails, and liquor remained prohibited throughout Cooke County until the 1990s and even, in some instances, beyond.[155]

Oklahoma also faced a number of restrictions, chiefly its own 1907 constitution, which had forbidden the sale and importation of "intoxicating liquors" such as whiskey. This provision was not changed after the federal prohibition ceased in 1933, except that Oklahoma did not classify beer as an alcoholic beverage.[156] Therefore, stores, bars, and restaurants across the Red River in Oklahoma developed a booming business, which was further enhanced in 1959, when voters approved the sale of all alcohols inside "package stores."[157] Hard liquors and spirits, however, still could not be consumed on-premises in Love County, Oklahoma until 2008, when voters elected to make the county completely wet.[158]

Johnny and Albina Schmitz's family retained the German business sense, work ethic, and sense of coziness. Schmitz descendants opened Club Schmitz, the popular beer and burger

---

[155] Denton Record Chronicle, September 6 1959; Gainesville Daily Register February 2013; Gainesville Register June 19 2015.
[156] Marietta Monitor, July 11 1958.
[157] Jimmie L. Franklin, "Prohibition." *The Encyclopedia of Oklahoma History and Culture.*
[158] Daily Oklahoma (Oklahoma City) January 9 2008.

joint on Old Denton Road (formerly U. S. 77) in Dallas that closed in 2014 after operating since 1946.[159] John Schmitz, now owner of the Stark Ranch, founded Select Energy to provide "engineering water solutions to the oil and gas industries."[160] He and his father worked the oil fields together.

The land that is Stark Ranch continues to be in good hands.

54. *Southern gate to Stark Ranch at what was the Brown's Ferry approach (Stark Ranch Collection).*

---

[159] Dallas Morning News December 19 2012; Dallas Observer, April 17 2014.
[160] Bloomberg Profile, John Schmitz.

Conclusion

The deep bend of the Red River is a major geographical feature. When looking at it from a satellite map, Love County, Oklahoma appears to be a peninsula. The bend's southern dip makes Gainesville (almost) a waterfront town. The high hills that flank the bend; the dense Cross Timbers that dot them; the concrete pillars from the old toll bridge still languishing in the water; the old roads that lead to the former ferry crossings; the springs of Pecan Creek and across the river at Brown's; and the remains of the pump station serve as permanent reminders that the land where Stark Ranch sits has influenced local, regional, and even national history.

It is a beautiful piece of land in a beautiful river valley. But it's not just nature and relics that make a place historic. It's the people, of course. They buried their dead, operated the ferries, built the bridges, drank from the spring, and used the river for food, water, transportation, and relaxation. Some were killed here, either by someone else's hands or by the swift currents. But the people who have lived at the deep bend of the Red River — the Wichitas, the Comanches, the Delawares, the

Stark Ranch of Cooke County, Texas: History that spans the Red River

Browns, the Sacras, the Roses, the Spires, Killgores, the Starks, the Shumachers, and the Schmitzes — have made indelible marks on the history of Cooke and Love Counties, and on Texas and Oklahoma.

While every piece of earth along the Red River has a story to tell, Stark Ranch's story, with its contributions to progress in the 19th and 20th century, is truly unique. Judging by the development happening all around the deep bend, with the trains, interstates, trucks, casinos, oil, pasture, and urbanization… its story is far from over.

> Look out for malaria. It is seasonable now. A few doses of Prickly Ash Bitters is a sure preventative. H. W. Stark Drug Co., Special Agents.

55. Advertisement for the H.W. Stark Drug Company in the Gainesville Daily Register, July 1915 (Newspapers.com).

56. Toll bridge at Sacra's Ferry, owned by the Gainesville Red River Bridge Company, erected in 1919 after congressional authorization in 1917, connected Oklahoma and Texas over the Red River at Stark Ranch (Morton Museum).

Wake Up.

The Cunningham Soap Works are doing a thriving business. The following grocers keep it in stock, from a bar to a box: J. T. Rowland, John King, G. W. Wayland, Wm. Kilgore, Maupin & Warren, Cobb & Pringle, S. Booth. Be sure and ask your grocer for the Egyptian Liquid Laundry Blueing. None better.

57. *Ad for a soap factory that includes the Killgore (Kilgore) store, Gainesville Daily Hesperian, 1890 (Newspapers.com).*

58. *Toll bridge ruins in the Red River with ferry crossing visible as seen from the Oklahoma side (Morton Museum).*

59. Clements Street in Gainesville used to be Grand Avenue, which connected the city to Sacra's Ferry. Today, this approach is no longer accessible (Stark Ranch Collection).

Sources

BOOKS

Debo, Angie (Editor). *The WPA Guide to Oklahoma*. Reprint. Wichita: University Press of Kansas, 1986.

Francaviglia, Richard. *The Cast Iron Forest: A natural and cultural History of the North American Cross Timbers*. Austin: UT Press, 1998.

Maguire, Jack. *Katy's Baby: The Story of Denison, Texas*. Fort Worth: Nortex Press, 1991.

Melugin, Ron. *Heroes, Scoundrels and Angels: Fairview Cemetery of Gainesville, Texas*. Charleston, SC: The History Press, 2010.

Robertson, John L. *Cooke County History, Past and Present*. Dallas: Cooke County Historical Society, 1992.

Tate, Juanita J. Keel. *Edmund Pickens (Okchantubby): First elected Chickasaw Chief, his Life and Times*. Ada, OK: Chickasaw Press, 2009.

CITY DIRECTORIES

Gainesville City Directory, 1910.
Gainesville City Directory, 1913.
Wichita Falls City Directory, 1934.

COMMUNICATIONS

Communication with Joseph Schmitz, December 27, 2020
Communication with Lucy Stark Sutton by Stark Ranch, July 13, 2016
Communication with Ray Nichols, November 30, 2020

GOVERNMENT ACTS AND RECORDS

1860 Census, tabulated. NARA with Familysearch.org
https://www2.census.gov/library/publications/decennial/1860/population/1860a-34.pdf?

49th Congress, Session 1, Chapters 354, 355. May 17, 1886.

59th Congress, Session 1, Chapter 1130. "An Act to regulate the

construction of bridges over navigable waters." March 23, 1906.
65th Congress Session 1 1917 Chapter 65. "An Act granting the consent of Congress to the Gainesville Red River Bridge
    Company to construct a bridge across Red River."
Chickasaw Indian Rolls #1790.
City of Gainesville, Texas. City directories.
City of Gainesville, Texas. Sanborn Maps. Perry Castaneda
    Library, UT-Austin.
City of Wichita Falls, Texas. City Directories.
Cooke County Deed Records. Deed of Trust 005, T.M King to
    H.Hulen trustee for Ed Sacra, 1876.
Cooke County Deed Records. Deed of Trust 004 p.521, 1912-1914.
Cooke County Deed records. Deed of Trust 2606, William
    Killgore and wife to Gainesville Bridge Company.
Cooke County Deed Records. Deed of Trust 6160, A. C. Rose and
    wife to William Killgore, July 20 1918.
Cooke County Probate Record. Probate 3197, 1923.
Curtis Act, 30 Stat. 495, c.517: "An Act for the Protection of the
    Indian Territory and for Other Purposes." 1898.
Dawes Act, 1889.
Love County records
Permit Law of the Chickasaw Nation, 1876.
Red River Authority Rules and Regulations, July 1960. City of
    Dallas Municipal Archives.
Testimony, Red River Bridge, 1930
Texas General Land Office. "Categories of Land Grants"
    https://www.glo.texas.gov/history/archives/forms/files/categories-of-land-grants.pdf 11/8/2020
Texas General Land Office. Fannin scrip: Brown & Taylor.

LETTERS AND MEMOS

C.C. Glenn to Members of the Board of Directors, Red River
    Valley Authority, 1960. City of Dallas Municipal Archives.

Henry Graeser to Robert Kerr, April 6 1959. City of Dallas Municipal Archives.
John Anderson to Henry Graeser March 10 1961. City of Dallas Municipal Archives.
K.H. Hoefle to W.S. McDonald. City of Dallas Memorandum, March 26 1954. City of Dallas Municipal Archives.

MAPS

United States Geological Maps, Indian Territory and Gainesville Quadrants, 1902.
United States Geological Maps, Sherman Quadrant, 1901.
Auto Trails Map, Rand McNally and Company, p. 408-409, 1924. David Rumsey Map Collection, Stanford University, CA.
Chickasaw Country, E. H. Ruffner, 1872. Fort Leavenworth, KS Military Division of the Missouri. Library of Congress.
Indian Territory, US Crops of Topographical Engineers, 1866. Library of Congress.
Indian Territory, G.W. & C.B. Colton & Co, 1869. David Rumsey Map Collection, Stanford University, CA.
Indian Territory, USGLO 1879. University of Texas, Arlington – Map Collections.
Map showing the Atchison, Topeka and Santa Fe railroad system with its connections. G.W. & C.B. Colton & Co, 1888. University of Texas, Arlington - Map Collections.
Map of Emigrant trail and Butterfield Trail, 1950s. University of Texas, Arlington - Map Collections.
Sanborn Fire Insurance Map of Gainesville, Texas, 1902. University of Texas, Austin – Perry Castaneda Library.
Texas, T. G. Bradford, 1835. University of Texas, Arlington – Map Collections.
Texas, Carl Christian Franz Radefeld, 1846. University of Texas, Arlington - Map Collections.
Texas, Henry Lange, ca. 1850s. University of Texas, Arlington – Map Collections.

Texas, J.H. Colton & Co, 1855. University of Texas, Arlington – Map Collections.
Texas, J.H. Colton, 1869. University of Texas, Arlington - Map Collections.
Texas, General Land Office, 1951. University of Texas, Arlington - Map Collections.
Texas, Styles-Goodrich, 1935. University of Texas, Arlington – Map Collections.

NEWSPAPERS
Ardmore Daily Press, November 4 1924.
Austin American Statesman, September 2 1874.
Austin American Statesman, September 5 1875.
Austin American Statesman, January 27 1885.
Austin American Statesman, January 1886.
Austin American Statesman, August 2 1930.
Austin American Statesman, January 31 1936.
Big Pasture News (Grandfield, Oklahoma) September 18 1925.
Blackwell Journal Tribune (Blackwell, OK), July 25 1931.
Cullison Banner, (Cullison, KS). September 30 1886.
Daily Ardmoreite, March 21 1894.
Daily Ardmoreite, July 11 1895.
Daily Ardmoreite, September 9 1910.
Daily Ardmoreite, September 14 1913.
Daily Ardmoreite, June 13 1916.
Daily Ardmoreite, February 9 1919.
Dallas Daily Herald, October 27 1858.
Dallas Daily Herald, July 13 1859.
Dallas Daily Herald, December 14 1859.
Dallas Daily Herald, October 6 1866.
Dallas Daily Herald, February 6 1869.
Dallas Morning News, September 5 1978.
Dallas Morning News. December 19 2012.
Dallas News March 17 1921.

Dallas Observer, April 17 2014.
Daily Oklahoman, July 17 1931.
Davis News (Davis, OK), March 17 1921.
Denison Daily News, December 9 1879.
Denton Record Chronicle, September 6 1959.
Enid Daily Eagle, June 10, 1918.
Fort Worth Daily Gazette, September 4 1887.
Fort Worth Daily Gazette, September 14 1887.
Fort Worth Daily Gazette, November 5 1886.
Fort Worth Daily Gazette, September 12 1886.
Fort Worth Daily Gazette, June 26 1885.
Fort Worth Daily Gazette, December 18 1888.
Fort Worth Daily Gazette, October 20 1886.
Fort Worth Daily Gazette April 1 1887.
Fort Worth Daily Gazette, January 9 1887.
Fort Worth Daily Gazette, January 11 1887.
Fort Worth Record Telegram, May 13 1916.
Fort Worth Record Telegram, October 19 1917
Fort Worth Record Telegram, November 1, 1917
Fort Worth Record Telegram, January 4 1929.
Fort Worth Star Telegram, November 14, 1930
Fort Worth Star Telegram, June 14 1931.
Fort Worth Star Telegram, July 19 1931.
Fort Worth Star Telegram, July 23 1931.
Fort Worth Star Telegram, July 24 1931.
Fort Worth Star Telegram, July 25 1931.
Fort Worth Star Telegram, July 26 1931.
Fort Worth Star Telegram, September 7 1931.
Fort Worth Star Telegram, August 26 1938.
Gainesville Daily Hesperian, September 3, 1888.
Gainesville Daily Hesperian, May 5 1894.
Gainesville Daily Hesperian, May 8 1888.
Gainesville Daily Hesperian, May 15 1888.
Gainesville Daily Hesperian, April 6 1897.

Gainesville Daily Hesperian, January 30 1889.
Gainesville Daily Hesperian, May 1 1889.
Gainesville Daily Hesperian, September 25 1889.
Gainesville Daily Hesperian, October 30 1891.
Gainesville Daily Register and Messenger, June 7 1916.
Gainesville Daily Register and Messenger, August 16 1917.
Gainesville Daily Register, July 20 1922.
Gainesville Daily Register, April 10 1923.
Gainesville Daily Register, December 22 2014.
Galveston Daily News, February 26, 1878.
Galveston Daily News, November 12 1879.
Galveston Daily News, April 29 1886.
Galveston Daily News, March 25, 1887.
Jacksboro News (Jacksboro, TX), October 24 1917.
Marietta Monitor (Marietta, OK), Oct 8 1915.
New Orleans Daily Crescent, April 13 1859.
Sweetwater Reporter (Sweetwater, TX), October 19 1952.
Vernon Record (Vernon, TX), April 7 1925.
Victoria Advocate (Victoria, TX), April 4 1928.
Texas Republican (Marshall, TX), November 12 1859.
Texas Republican (Marshall, TX), December 18 1868.
The Times (Shreveport, LA), June 16 1908.
The Times (Shreveport, LA), July 21 1927.
Weekly Harald (Marshall, TX), July 11 1876.
Weekly Republican Traveler (Arkansas City, KS), September 4 1886.

ONLINE
Ancestry.com
Bloomberg Profile. "John Schmitz."
https://www.bloomberg.com/profile/person/17362315
Texas Ecoregions. "Grand Prairie and Plains."
http://texastreeid.tamu.edu/content/texasEcoRegions/GrandPrairiePlains/

The Encyclopedia of Oklahoma History and Culture. "Flipper, Henry Ossian," by Theodore D. Harris.
https://www.okhistory.org/publications/enc/entry.php?entry=FL002.
Oklahoma Department of Transportation. "Memorial Highways: U.S. 77." https://www.odot.org/memorial/highways/htmls/us77.htm
Oklahoma History Center.
https://www.okhistory.org/shpo/contexts/Region4&5NativeAmericanPt3.pdf
Rootsweb.ancestry.com. "Samuel A. Brown."
www.rootsweb.ancestry.com/~okttp/history/volume_4/samuel_a_brown.htm

ORAL HISTORIES
Indian Pioneer Papers, 1937: Lillie Sprowls, R. L. Nichols, Dixie Colbert, W.R. Mulkey, Jennie Selfridge.
Leeper Lake, oral history of John Mahan, 1944.

Stark Ranch of Cooke County, Texas: History that spans the Red River

INDEX

3rd Texas Mounted Volunteers, Civil War 25
25th Infantry Division, Korea 111
27th Infantry Regiment, Korea 111
49th Congress, 1886 5, 46, 66, 67, 119,
59th Congress, 1906 65, 119
65th Congress, 1917 5, 69, 120
Abilene Cattle Trail (Chisholm Trail) 39-41, 84
Abolition 29-33
Adelsverein 109
Addington Bend, Oklahoma 20
Addington Ranch 22
African-American 31
Anglo-American (European-American) 17, 19, 24, 25, 30, 31, 37-39, 49, 50, 52, 87
Alabama 21, 31, 38
Altus, Oklahoma 84
An Act granting… Gainesville Red River Bridge Company, 1917, 5, 69, 120
An Act to regulate… construction of bridges, 1906 65, 119
Ardmore, Oklahoma 45, 55
Arkansas 10, 11, 24, 31,63, 73
Arkansas River 65, 114
Arthur City, Texas 87
Atchison, Topeka and Santa Fe Railway 11, 27, 121
Aylesworth, Oklahoma 100
Baer's Ferry on Red River 100
Big Mineral Creek 100
Bird's Fort 42
Bismark, Otto von 109
Bison 16, 26,31, 36, 37, 52, 53, 38
Bohemia 111
Bootleggers 26, 111
Bonnie & Clyde 87
Borderlands 9, 34, 35, 39, 52, 53, 58,71
Bourland, James 25, 32, 33
Brown, A.W. 18
Brown, Alfred P. 54

Brown, J.C. 44
Brown, Samuel (S. H.) 4, 10, 18, 19, 43, 115
Brown, Tom 54
Brown's Ferry on the Red River 20, 44-47, 49, 51, 53, 55, 61, 66-67, 70, 74, 77, 85, 86, 103, 113, 114
Brown's Spring (Refuge Spring) 4, 10, 18, 19, 22, 44, 47, 48, 50
Brown's Spring Cemetery 19, 20,47
Bryan County, Oklahoma 20
Buffalo Bayou, Brazos & Colorado Railway 43, 57
Burkburnett, Texas 84, 88
Burneyville Ferry on the Red River 39, 86
Butterfield Overland Stage Coach and Mail Company 20, 26, 27, 29, 35, 121
Byers, Texas 84
Caddo (tribe, nation) 14-16, 25
Cahokia 14
Canada 9
Canadian River 14, 41, 65
Canadian River Valley Bridge & Construction Company 66, 68
cattle 11, 20, 37-41, 51, 52, 55, 104
Chicago 58-60
Chickasaw Bridge Company 5, 46, 66
Chickasaw Nation 4, 10, 2-22, 26, 39, 40, 44-46, 49, 50, 52, 53, 55, 58, 65, 80, 86, 89
Chickasha, Oklahoma 39
Chief Big Tree 34
Chisholm, Jesse 41
Chisholm Trail (Abilene Cattle Trail) 39, 40
Choctaw Nation 21, 22, 58
Churches 30, 31, 77, 78, 109-111
Civil War (U.S., 1861-1865) 19, 25, 27-28, 31-33, 37, 38, 41, 43, 57, 72, 77, 80, 81, 109
Clay County, Texas 36, 85
Cloud, Ike (Isaac) 38,79
Cloud-Stark House 5, 79
Cloud Ranch 22, 38,41
Club Schmitz 113
Colbert, Benjamin 20, 65, 89

Colbert, Frank 89
Colbert, Oklahoma 19, 65, 89
Colbert Toll Bridge 6, 65, 89
Colbert's Ferry on the Red River 20, 23, 35, 46, 69
Comanches (tribe, nation) 10, 15, 16, 25, 34, 109, 114
Commerce Street, Gainesville 73, 74
Confederate Conscription Act, 1862 33
Courtney Ferry on the Red River 86
Criner family 19, 46-48
Criner Hills, Oklahoma 47
Cross Timbers 4, 13-16, 36, 71, 80, 109, 114
Curtis Act, 1898   39
Dallas, Texas 35, 42, 54, 57, 60, 62, 92, 101, 103-107, 113
Davidson, Oklahoma 88
Davis, Oklahoma 55
Dawes Severality Act, 1887   46, 49
Deep bend of the Red River 20, 36, 42, 43, 47, 48, 51-53, 70-72, 77, 78, 80, 100, 114, 115
De la Harpe, Bernard 116
Delaware Bend, Texas 4, 14, 23, 86, 87
Delaware Bend Ferry on the Red River 86,24
Delaware River Valley 23
Delaware Tribe/Nation 23, 86
De Mezieres, Athanase 17
Democrat Party 31, 100
Denison Dam 100
Denison and Pacific Railway 59-61
Denison and Southeastern Railway 59
Denison, Texas 23, 35, 46, 58-61, 84, 85, 88, 89, 91, 94, 97, 100
Denton County, Texas 34, 42, 101
Denton, Texas 61
Desalination 105, 107
Dick, Hal 87
Dobson, A. E. 66
Doss, S. M. 30
Dougherty, Oklahoma (Strawberry Flats) 63
Dougherty, W. M. 66

drought on Red River 11, 14, 101
Dunham, J. S. H. 62
Dust Bowl 101
Dye Street, Gainesville (Weaver Street) 46
Elm Fork of the Trinity River 99, 102, 104
Fairview Cemetery, Gainesville 77
Fannin County, Texas 39, 84, 86, 100
Fannin Scrip 51
Fischer, Abalonia (Apalonia) 111
Fish Creek 14, 34, 101
Fleetwood Ranch 22
Flipper, Henry O. 36
floods on Red River 14, 53, 65, 85, 87, 89, 99, 100, 104, 105
Flusche, Emil 109
Flusche, August 109
Ford, L. M. 10, 43, 51
fords on Red River 39, 86
Fort Arbuckle 20, 26
Fort Belknap 60, 26
Fort Fitzhugh 20
Fort Sill 36, 109
Fort Washita 20
Fort Worth, Texas 60, 61, 64, 93, 99
Freeman's Ferry on the Red River 86
Frontier (troubles, depredations) 20, 25, 26, 31, 34, 60, 71
Gainesville and Chickasaw Bridge Company 5, 66
Gainesville, Henrietta and Western Railway 60
Gainesville-Marietta bridge 92
Gainesville Red River Bridge Company 69-70, 72, 74, 88, 92, 93, 95, 97, 116
Gainesville to Ardmore Highway 83, 92
Galveston, Texas 61, 108
Garza-Little Elm Reservoir 107
German 108-110
Glass Creek 100
Goodlett, Texas 85
Good Roads Movement 82, 86
Graeser, Henry 105

Graham, J.C. 48
Grand Avenue, Gainesville 51, 71, 118
Grandfield, Oklahoma 84
Grapevine Lake 101, 107
Grayson County, Texas 20, 24, 32, 34, 52, 55, 58, 65, 72, 75, 77, 86
grazing rights 39
Great Hanging 32,34
Great Southwest Strike, 1887 62
Greenville, Texas 59
Gulf, Colorado, and Santa Fe Bridge 62, 61
Gulf, Colorado and Santa Fe Railway 61, 62, 64, 66, 99
Hagerman, Texas 100
Henderson County, Texas 30
Hobby Highway 11, 84, 92
Hobbs Ferry on the Red River 86
Holder, Lucile 75
Hollis, Oklahoma 85
Horton, Maggie Holder Killgore 75-77
Horton, Val 75
Horton, William 75
Houston and Texas Central Railway 23, 35, 57, 58
Houston, Texas 35
Hubert H. Moss Lake 14, 101
Humphries, George 29, 30
H.W. Stark Drug Company, Gainesville 77, 78, 116
Injunction 88-91, 93
Illinois 40, 109
Illinois Bend, Texas 84
Indiana 24, 31
Indianapolis 72
Indian Removal Act, 1830 21
Indian Trail 26, 36
Iowa 92, 109-111,
James, Jesse 87
Jefferson Highway 90
Jefferson County, Oklahoma 16, 40, 95
Johnny's B-29 Bar 111

Johnny's DX Truck Stop 111
K Company, 22nd Confederate Cavalry 72
Kansas 13, 16, 29, 30, 41
Kansas City, Missouri 35, 61, 69, 103
Kansas-Nebraska Act, 1854 30
Kansas-Oklahoma-Texas Highway 84
Kellner Jetty Company 103
Kentucky 21, 24, 31
Kerr, Robert S. 105
Killgore Department Store 66, 75
Killgore, Mary Dobson 72-75
Killgore, William (Kilgore) 11, 66, 68, 72-78, 80, 81
Kiowa (tribe, nation) 10, 15, 34, 38, 109
King of Trails Highway 90
King, T. M. 51
Lake Dallas 101, 102, 107
Lake Fork 107
Lake Lavon 101
Lake Ray Hubbard 101
Lake Tawakoni 107
Lake Texoma 99, 100
Lakes to Gulf Highway 92
Leeper, J. D. 48, 68, 70
Leeper Lake 48
Lewisville Lake 101, 107
Lindsay, Texas 66, 110
Lindsey, J. M. 61
Little Mineral Creek 100
Littleton, C. C. 68
liquor 26, 111, 112
Longview, Texas 57
Louisiana Purchase 10, 17, 90
Louisiana Territory 9, 30
Love County, Oklahoma 6, 10, 18, 20, 31, 63, 68, 81, 111, 112, 114
Love Ranch 22
Love Valley, Oklahoma 22, 27
Loy, J. J. 94, 95

Mages, Theresa Bayer 111
Mahan, John 48, 68
Marrietta, Oklahoma 97
Marshall, Texas 29, 57
Maudlin, G. M. 76
Mexican-American War, 1846-1848 25, 32
Mexican Texas 9, 23
Mexico 9, 30, 39, 52, 78
McCoy, Joseph 40, 41
McKemie, William 68
McLish Ranch 22
Midland Bridge Company 69
Mineola, Texas 59
Minnesota 109
Mississippi 20, 21, 38
Mississippi River 10, 14, 23, 65, 99
Missouri 24, 31, 58, 77, 109
Missouri Compromise, 1820 30
Missouri, Kansas and Texas Railway 35, 58-61
Mitchell, H. F. 68
Moonshining (moonshiners) 11, 20, 26, 85
Moss Lake 14, 101
Moutry Duck Lake (Leeper Lake) 48
Muenster, Texas 109-112
Murray, William "Alfalfa Bill" 90, 91, 94
Natchitoches, Louisiana 16, 117
National Bridge Company 65
Native American 14, 16, 17, 23, 31, 32, 34
New Deal 100
New Spain 9, 10
New York 24, 29
Nichols, R. L. 37
North Texas Highway 84
Ohio River Valley 23
Okchantubby (Edmund Pickens) 22
Oklahoma City 66, 93
Oklahoma National Guard 91

Old Denton Road, Dallas 113
Overton, Benjamin 49, 52, 55
Overton, Charles 55
package stores 112
Palmer, E. C. 29, 30
Panola County (Choctaw Nation) 65
Parker, William 77
Parker, Una Stark Anderson 77
Parilla, Diego Ortiz 16
Pecan Creek 24, 34, 101-104, 114
permit fee/permit law 4, 49, 50
Peter's Colony 24, 25, 42, 110
Petrolia, Texas 84
Phoenix Bridge Company 63
Pickens County (Chickasaw Nation) 22, 31, 47, 63, 80, 110
Pickens, Edmund (Okchantubby) 22
Porter family 34
Pottsboro, Texas 55
Preemption 4, 5, 32, 43, 50, 54
Preston, Texas (Preston Bend) 39, 84, 100
Preston-Woodville Bridge 88
Prohibition 112
Prussia 111
Quanah, Texas 84
Quantrill, William 87
Ranching 22, 24, 37, 38, 41, 44, 49, 52, 53
Rayburn, Sam 69, 100, 101
Reconstruction 37
Red River Bridge Company 20, 46, 88-92, 94, 97
Red River Bridge War, 1931 89
Red River City, Texas 23, 35, 58, 65
Red River Pump Station 6, 11, 101-105, 107, 114
Red River Station, Texas 41 84
Red River Valley Authority 6, 105, 106
Red River Wars, 1874-1875 109
Refuge Spring (Brown's Spring) 4, 10, 18, 19, 22, 44, 47, 48, 50
Republic of Texas 9, 23, 42, 52

Ringgold, Texas 84, 97
Rock Bluff Ferry on the Red River 86
Rock Creek 100
Rollins, R. S. 61
Roosevelt, Franklin Delano 100
Rose, A. C. 55, 74, 115
Rose, Hettie 55, 74, 115
S. H. 40 92, 93, 96
Sacra, Ed 10, 51, 52
Sacra, James 55
Sacra, Mattie Carter Overton 5, 51, 52
Sacra, Richard 55
Sacra's Ferry on the Red River 6, 51, 66, 68-71, 74, 83, 85, 86, 89, 116, 118
Safety bicycle 82
San Bernardo and San Teodoro 17
San Diego, California 26
Santa Fe, New Mexico 61
Schmitz, Albina Mages 111, 113
Schmitz, Catherine Neu 110
Schmitz, John Henry 110, 111
Schmitz, John William 110
Schmitz, Mary Bezner 110
Schmitz, William Joseph 109, 110
Scott-Leeper Company 48
Select Energy 113
Selfridge, Jennie 44
Senate Bill No. 75, 1929   88
Sharecropping 73
Shawnee (tribe, nation) 23
Shawneetown, Grayson County 58
Shawnee Trail (Texas Cattle Road) 41
Shawnee War, 1811 23
Sherman, Texas 26, 35, 58
Sherwood, F. H. 68
Shreveport, Louisiana 57
Shumacher family 79, 115
Sivell's Bend, Texas 41

slavery 21, 28, 30, 31
Smith, David 62
Smith, Will 44, 54
South Fish Creek Battle, 1863 34
Sowell's Bluff, Texas 84
Spires, Cicero 74
Spiro 14
Sprowls, Lillie 19, 49, 50
Squatting 41, 43, 49
St. Louis, Missouri 14, 26, 58
Stone, Will 54
Sugg Ranch 22
Sullivan, C. F. 94, 95
Stark, Harlen W. (H.W.) 11, 74, 77-80
Stark, Katie Miller 77, 78
Stark, Lucy Spires Killgore 11, 72-81, 101, 107-108
Sterling, Ross 90, 91
Taovaya (tribe) 16, 17
Tarrant, Edward 42
Taylor, R. W. 44, 51
Telephone, Texas 84
Tennessee 21, 24, 31, 32, 72, 75
Tennessee River Valley Authority 100
Terral Bridge Company 95
Terral, Oklahoma 19
Terrell, George W. 42
Texanna, Oklahoma 19
Texas and Pacific Railway 57
Texas Christian University 77
Texas fever 41
Texas Highway Commission 90, 91, 95
Texas Rangers 20, 25, 91
Texas Cattle Road (Shawnee Trail) 41
Texas Troubles 29
Texas Western Railroad Company 57
Thacker, Zachariah 63
Thackerville, Oklahoma 19, 47, 54, 63

Tillman County, Oklahoma 88
Tishomingo, Oklahoma 22
toll bridges 5, 6, 20, 65-69, 72, 79, 85, 81-92, 94-98, 100, 114, 116, 117
toll rates 70, 89, 90, 95
Treaty of Hidalgo, 1848   30
Treaty of Old Town, 1818   21
Tuck's Ferry on the Red River 86
Tuck, Cuburt 86
Tuck, John 86
Twenty Negro Law, 1862   33
Union League (Lincoln League) 33, 34
Union Pacific Railway, Southern Branch 58
U. S 75   92
U. S. 77   93, 96, 98, 111, 113, 114
Vernon, Texas 84
Walnut Bend, Texas 41
Walterscheid family 110
Warren, Abel 20, 86
Washita River 84, 63, 100
Washington Ranch 44
Waskom, Texas 57
Weaver Street, Gainesville (Dye Street) 46
Weaver, William Thomas Green 35
Wells Fargo Express Company 74
Western Cattle Trail 84
Westphalia, Germany 109
Westphalia, Iowa 111
Whaley, J. C. 68
Whiskey Trail 36, 111
Whitesboro, Texas 59, 60
White Rock Lake 101
White Steamer (automobile) 79
Whitewright, Texas 59
Wichita (tribe, nation) 10, 15, 16, 25, 42, 114
Wichita County (Choctaw Nation) 22
Wichita County, Texas 88
Wichita Falls, Texas 77

Wichita Mountains 17
Wilson, Woodrow 83
Winstar Casino 80
Wisconsin 109, 111
Wolfhounds (Korean War) 111
Woodville, Oklahoma 84, 100
Works Progress Administration (WPA) 39, 44, 48, 50
World War I/ Great War 72, 82, 100
World War II 75
Young County, Texas 25, 60
Young, William C. 25, 32, 33

About the Author

John Schmitz was born in Gainesville, Texas to John Henry and Albina Schmitz in 1960. He grew up participating in running his family's beer joint across the river in Thackerville, Oklahoma and, at seventeen, opened his own store. After graduating high school in Lindsay, John started working in the oil fields. By the age of twenty-three, he founded his first (but not his last!) company geared towards the oil industry. The same year as he began his entrepreneurial career — which would include owning, acquiring, and selling several companies— he married his high school sweetheart, Sandy Hermes. In the ensuing forty years they had three daughters, Tiffany, Shelby, and Suzanne, and now enjoy their two grandchildren, Lucy and Henry. John and Sandy currently reside north of Gainesville at the Stark Ranch on the Red River.

Stark Ranch of Cooke County, Texas: History that spans the Red River

Red River Historian Press
History where the South meets the West
www.redriverhistorian.com

For over twenty years, the Red River Historian has been researching, documenting, and sharing the history of the Red River Valley that runs between Texas, Oklahoma, Arkansas, and Louisiana – where the South meets the West – through books, presentations, websites, videos, consulting, and more.

Traveling History with Bonnie & Clyde: Complete Itineraries for retracing the Gangster-Era Southwest

Traveling History up the Cattle Trails: A Road Tripper's Guide to the Cattle Drives of the Southwest

Traveling History among the Ghosts: Abandoned Places in the Red River Valley

The Stark Ranch of Cooke County, Texas: History that Spans the Red River

Shop for books and more at www.redriverhistorian.com

www.ingramcontent.com/pod-product-compliance
Lightning Source LLC
Chambersburg PA
CBHW072202100526
44589CB00015B/2327